New Thought, Ancient Wisdom

New Thought, Ancient Wisdom

THE HISTORY AND FUTURE OF THE NEW THOUGHT MOVEMENT

Glenn R. Mosley

TEMPLETON FOUNDATION PRESS
PHILADELPHIA · LONDON

Templeton Foundation Press
300 Conshohocken State Road, Suite 670
West Conshohocken, PA 19428
www.templetonpress.org

*Templeton Foundation Press helps intellectual leaders and others learn
about science research on aspects of realities, invisible and intangible.
Spiritual realities include unlimited love, accelerating creativity, worship,
and the benefits of purpose in persons and in the cosmos.*

Library of Congress Cataloging-in-Publication Data
Mosley, Glenn.
  New Thought, ancient wisdom : the history and future of the New
Thought movement / Glenn R. Mosley.
     p. cm.
  Includes bibliographical references (p.) and index.
  ISBN-13: 978-1-59947-089-4 (pbk. : alk. paper)
  ISBN-10: 1-59947-089-6 (pbk. : alk. paper) 1. Unity School of
Christianity. 2. New Thought. I. Title.
  BX9890.U54M67 2006
  299'.93—dc22
                                            2005028771

Printed in the United States of America
06 07 08 09 10 10 9 8 7 6 5 4 3 2 1

Designed and typeset by Gopa & ted2, Inc.

To Martha, with great admiration for all I know about you
and with great love, for all I know about you and
for knowing I will never know all about you.

Contents

Foreword

ANY RELIGIOUS MOVEMENT that endures for 250 years or more gathers a considerable body of literature around it. Certainly that is true of the New Thought movement. Its various strands influence the thinking and, perhaps more important, the development of spirituality for millions of people throughout the world who may be unaware of the sources of their feelings of newfound peace and inspiration. The printed word has always been a vital part of the New Thought and Ancient Wisdom outreach. Today a bibliography of the movement would include many thousands of books and hundreds of thousands of issues of various periodicals.

Thus, it might seem that there is not much need for another book about New Thought. But Glenn Mosley's new book about the movement focuses on certain aspects and the particular genius of several of the founders and leaders of the movements and ministries that comprise New Thought. For example, from Unity literature Mosley focuses on Charles Fillmore's metaphysical treatment of the Bible and Charles and Myrtle Fillmore's power of the spoken word. From Religious Science literature, he focuses on Ernest Holmes's great teaching genius in written form. Mosley also incorporates a chronology of New Thought that encompasses well more than two and a half centuries.

Through *New Thought, Ancient Wisdom*, Mosley reveals intricacies of paths which modern people have repeated to their benefit and others may continue to replicate and thereby find new strength, peace of mind, and a rekindled spirituality. As the title suggests, its path leads to New Thought and ancient wisdom.

Finally, my friend and colleague on the quest, Glenn Mosley, includes modern-day, scientific research results regarding spirituality, prayer, and health being conducted by major universities, medical research facilities, and hospitals. Such research efforts are encouraged and often receive grants from the John Templeton Foundation.

It seems to me that for a serious student of Truth as presented through *New Thought, Ancient Wisdom*, this volume will inevitably become an essential part of a working library.

Sir John Templeton

Acknowledgments

THIS LOOK AT THE PAST, present, and future of the New Thought, Ancient Wisdom movement is possible because of the assistance of many people whom I wish to thank. Of necessity many shall remain unnamed, but some merit special mention. I would like to thank my doctoral advisor and life mentor, Dr. Eugene Bahn, who insisted that I not leave New Thought ministry when I considered it, and my wife, Martha, for being there when I made time to write when I didn't have time to write. My thanks also to another friend and colleague, Reverend Rebekah Dunlap, for her great ideas, suggestions, editing, and other assistance in bringing this book to the light of day.

Through the kindness of the Unity School of Christianity's Heritage Library, I have been able to use critical reviews, memorabilia, books, and articles by and about Charles and Myrtle Fillmore and Unity. Also, thanks to Unity School for permission to publish Charles Fillmore's transcripts that appear in appendix C. Through the assistance of friends and colleagues in other New Thought movements, I have also delved into other recent and distant past progenitors of modern-day New Thought, ancient wisdom, including Ernest Holmes and the Science of the Mind, the writings of Emanuel Swedenborg, Phineas Parkhurst Quimby, Ralph Waldo Emerson, E. B. Weeks, Emma Curtis Hopkins, Johnnie Colemon, Fenwicke Holmes, Masahauru Taniguchi, Nona Brooks, and others.

Finally, my personal thanks to Sir John Templeton and to Joanna Hill of the Templeton Foundation and my colleagues at the Foundation in their research of the implications of the future relationship of science and religion, as well as science, religion, and health, both physical and mental. My deep appreciation to all for their assistance in bringing *New Thought, Ancient Wisdom* to readers across numerous disciplines.

Introduction

THE SCOPE of a human soul, its life's work and accomplishments, can be immense. In the earth-time dimension of a variety of experiences and teachings, many apparent opposites and complementary events often find composition and expression. Great teachings can uplift humanity and raise the level of human consciousness. The truth of one's spiritual self can be discovered through the pathway of everyday life. Doors may open, opportunities occur, and the aspirant can embark on a process of discovery and, ultimately, recognize a great truth—that he or she is a significant expression in the universe!

Charles Fillmore, cofounder of the Unity School of Christianity, was convinced that it was possible for all men and women to achieve the same level of consciousness attained by Jesus. He emphasized that the *purpose* of life was not about creating wealth or acquiring material goods, but about *living* the Christ life. The acceptance that Unity offers and its emphasis on continuing spiritual growth often provide a healing change from a competitive, judgmental religious environment. This attitude makes it possible for people to learn from many sources. In fact, the name "Unity" suggests values of kinship that underlie all faiths.

Several historical studies of both Charles Fillmore and Unity School of Christianity exist, thereby providing us with considerable insight into Fillmore's rhetoric, life, and education, and into the development of Unity School. Four important biographical and historical volumes have been written: one by Unity's poet laureate, James Dillet Freeman, and the other three by outside chroniclers Marcus Bach, Hugh D'Andrade, and Neal Vahle. The most notable dissertation is that of Rudolph F. Verderber at the University of Missouri.[1] However, they did not focus on an analysis of the development of Fillmore's interpretation of biblical literature, nor did they focus on an evaluation of Unity's *spoken word* phenomenon. The Vahle study included the entire movement by discussion of the growth of some one thousand Unity ministries and the Association of Unity Churches, International.

Besides the volumes of Fillmore's works, the biographical treatises about Fillmore, and the histories of Unity already cited, chapters and large sections of many other articles and books are concerned with Fillmore and Unity. Such works include those by religious researcher and psychologist Frank S. Mead, Dr. Gina Cerminara, and two works by Charles S. Braden, professor of religious history at Southern Methodist University. Considerable assistance is also derived from *A Complete Concordance to the Published Writings of Charles Fillmore*, compiled by Jeffrey Fischer.[2]

In addition to the foregoing volumes, Fillmore devoted considerable attention to the *spoken word* tradition in the other eight books published during his life, in the three books compiled and published posthumously, and in innumerable signed articles published in seven periodicals from 1889 to 1948. Other Unity pioneers, as well as modern Unity writers, also offer considerable insight into the *spoken word* tradition: foremost among them being H. Emilie Cady, Myrtle Fillmore, and Clara May Rowland.

Authenticity is a problem when evaluating speech texts in history.[3] Even though verbatim manuscripts exist, the *way* a word is spoken and emphasized often is as important as the word itself; for example, the "Oh!" of surprise and the "Oh!" of disappointment are not always clearly discernable in speech manuscripts. Two of Fillmore's thirteen books do much to obviate the problem of *who* said *what*. *Talks on Truth* is an edited-for-print version of fourteen talks he gave prior to 1926. In another, larger volume, the *Metaphysical Bible Dictionary,* Fillmore wrote his principles for the student's use in interpreting Scriptures.[4]

The first section of this book is directed toward the description and evaluation of the theories and methods of biblical interpretation Charles Fillmore developed. We will investigate Unity's unique approach to the interpretation of biblical literature, both through silent and spoken reading. In addition, illumination on the effect of speaking words of prayer aloud and in a specified manner will be offered.[5]

We will also consider additional pioneers in the New Thought movement, many of whom were contemporaries of Charles and Myrtle Fillmore. These great souls, such as Ernest Holmes, founder of the Science of Mind; Mary Baker Eddy, founder of the Church of Christ, Scientist; Ralph Waldo Trine, philosopher, mystic, teacher, and early mentor of New Thought; Joel Goldsmith, founder of "The Infinite Way;" and other New Thought leaders contributed works that contain the distilled wisdom of several eras and many cultures. (See appendix D for a listing of early New Thought movement participants.) Modern proponents of New Thought activities certainly include Johnnie Colemon, founder of the Universal Foundation for Better Living in Chicago; Dr. Barbara King, founder of Hillside International Chapel of Truth in Atlanta; and Michael Beckwith, D.D., founder and Spiritual Director of Agape International Spiritual Center in Culver City, California.

We will look at how Unity shares with other members of the New Thought movement many of the same guiding principles that help position the soul for coping with daily earth living. These principles include centrality of mind, focus upon the eminence of the Divine (God) within, metaphysical healing, and the clear distinction between Jesus the Christ and Jesus, the man of history.

One perspective for this study is to provide an explanation of the procedures and the functions of metaphysical Bible interpretation and the specific prayer process known as the *spoken word*. It is hoped that as a by-product of the study, the reader will arrive at an awareness of the worth of these two branches of Unity. It is, therefore, my intention to answer at least some of the justifiable questions that students ask about the Bible's *relevance*.

Another perspective is to review the various strands of the New Thought movement and look at some of the major impacts it has had regarding the development of spirituality for millions of people throughout the world. As we look at the changing faces of reality in today's world, we can consider areas for researching present and future spiritual needs.

Inasmuch as we are living in what some term "a scientific age," it also seems relevant to review some of the surprising shifts that seem to be occurring at the beginning of this century, especially the effects they may be having on the growth of the soul. As scientific realism is going through a transition, so does theology seem to be experiencing a healthy reassessment of theological doctrines. We now know that the incredible events of evolution and the extraordinarily complex origin of life are punctuated with quite miraculous emergent considerations. There can be some meaningful and beneficial future areas of interaction between religion and science. Perhaps we can ask the question: Does religion offer a whole new realm to be scientifically explored? What could discoveries in this area mean to the global positioning of the soul? As Ernest Holmes stated, "We all look forward to the day when science and religion shall walk hand in hand through the visible to the invisible."[6]

Because one of the focuses of this study is transcending the limits of ordinary consciousness, it is urgent that we humans take a look at where we are headed in the twenty-first century. What are the spiritual tools we need as individuals for greater clarity, uncompromising integrity, deep compassion, and divine love? How may we understand and utilize our role in the interconnected human system of life? Can this book serve as a stimulus for your own personal experience of living a greater manifest self?

Much of the source material for our exploration of the relationship between science and religion in the twenty-first century derives from work accomplished by the John Templeton Foundation in Conshohocken, Pennsylvania. One of the great steps Sir John Templeton made in his spiritual journey was the establishing of this Foundation in 1987 to explore and encourage the relationship between science and religion. It brings together scientists, theologians, medical professionals, philosophers, philanthropists, and other scholars to plan programs and help publish the tremendous opportunities for new spiritual information through research.[7]

New Thought, Ancient Wisdom

The Fillmores and the Origins of the Unity Movement

1

Charles Fillmore's Youth, Education, and Early Work

CHARLES FILLMORE was born on an Indian reservation on the Sauk River, near the small town of St. Cloud, Minnesota, at 4 A.M. on August 22, 1854.[1] His father, Henry Fillmore, a native of Buffalo, New York, was a second cousin of Millard Fillmore, the thirteenth president of the United States. As an adult, Henry moved to the Minnesota wilderness and became a trader with the Chippewa Indians.

Mary Georgiana Stone, who would become Charles's mother, was a Canadian of English and Welsh ancestry. Her family moved to Minnesota when she was a child. Years later, she often related her wilderness experiences to her son. He recalled:

> My mother often told us of her hair-raising experiences alone much of the time among roving bands of Chippewa and Sioux Indians, who were nearly always on the warpath, not only with each other, but sometimes with the whites. One day when Father had gone to another trading post on the east side of the Mississippi River and she was alone in the cabin, a band of Sioux dashed up, grabbed me out of her arms, and rode off. She was, of course, nearly distracted but could do nothing. At sundown they brought me back unharmed. Such incidents made my early years romantic but crude and unprofitable.[2]

In the same frontier country, two years after Charles's birth, another son, Norton, was born. When Charles was seven his parents separated. In self-imposed exile, Henry Fillmore built a hut for himself in the forest some ten miles north of the family cabin. According to biographer Hugh D'Andrade:

Henry Fillmore, it seemed, was a "solitary," one of those migrants who came to the West to seek a place removed from the haunts of their fellowmen, and not merely to find a new and promising environment. After the glamour of a new experience had passed, such men often withdrew from society. They liked loneliness and regarded a solitary life as their prerogative. Usually the society in which they moved accepted their way of life without censure.[3]

The little family of three—Mary, Charles, and Norton—managed to survive on their own. Cranberries growing at the water's edge often froze beneath the winter ice. Charles and Norton would break the ice of a nearby pond or stream to find and gather these berries or to fish. Wild game was also plentiful. Like the Indians of the territory, during the fall young Charles harvested wild rice in a canoe by bending the rice blades over his canoe and beating the grain with a stick until it fell off. He then took the rice home to dry and store in preparation for the long, forty-degrees-below-zero Minnesota winter that lay ahead.[4]

At the age of ten, Charles dislocated his hip while skating and was confined to his home. Doctors diagnosed rheumatism in the right leg, which gradually developed into tuberculosis of the hip. Many abscesses penetrated to the bones of both legs, and, eventually, both arms as well. After a two-year struggle, during which the illness progressed and regressed, he was finally able to move about with assistance from crutches and a cane and could return to school. He attended classes off and on until he was eighteen. The school convened for only three months in mid-winter, which made walking there with crutches extremely difficult.

Charles's brother Norton ran away from home, never to return to the bleakness that was St. Cloud, Minnesota, when Charles was about twelve. Mary and her chronically ill son grew closer, sharing two struggles: his physical ailments and their mutual economic survival.

Charles went to work in St. Cloud when he was fourteen. As a printer's apprentice, known then colloquially as a "devil," he swept floors, cleaned type, and operated a hand press. This work profoundly influenced his later career. During his apprenticeship, Charles developed a close friendship with Edgar Taylor, a young man his own age. Edgar's mother, Caroline Taylor, had attended Oberlin College and was tutoring her son. Since she liked her son's companion, she taught Charles as well. Of Caroline Taylor's influence, D'Andrade reports:

> [S]he introduced Charles to advanced ideas which were raising eyebrows in New England. Bronson Alcott was questioning old theological beliefs. Ralph Waldo Emerson had retired from his pastorate because he could not agree with some of the theological ideas he was expected to promulgate from the pulpit. In New England, transcendentalism was coming to birth; agnosticism was gaining ground. Robert Ingersoll was delivering lectures deemed heretical by churchgoers. Caroline Taylor did not conceal such original ideas from her young pupil, so Charles Fillmore learned to ask searching questions about orthodox theology when he was still in his teens.[5]

It was also under Mrs. Taylor's tutelage that Charles came to love the writings of Tennyson, Shelley, Shakespeare, the Brownings, James Russell Lowell, and Ralph Waldo Emerson.[6]

Mrs. Taylor's influence, his friendship with Edgar, and his job as a printer's "devil" served as diversion and instruction, but Charles grew restless and wanted other surroundings. At age nineteen, he traveled to Caddo, a small town in Indian Territory just north of the Texas border. He stayed for only a short time before moving on to Denison, Texas, where he obtained a job as a freight clerk with the Missouri, Kansas, and Texas Railway. Charles sent for his mother and they built a home in Denison, where he lived for five years. His mother lived with him for the rest of her life.

While still in Denison, it was at a literary and philosophic group meeting, which met in private homes and where poetry was often read aloud, that Charles Fillmore's life changed. It was there that he met a red-haired schoolteacher from Clinton, Missouri, named Myrtle Page.[7] In 1881, five years after their meeting, they were married.

During the time he was courting Myrtle, Fillmore moved from Texas and became a mining assayer in Gunnison, Colorado. When the mining boom broke, in a kind of nomadic way, the new couple moved from Gunnison to Pueblo, Colorado, where he began working in real estate. Sons Lowell Page (named for James Russell Lowell) and Waldo Rickert (for Ralph Waldo Emerson) were born in 1882 and 1884, respectively.

In characteristic dissatisfaction with his surroundings and his work, and with the urge to go elsewhere, but with no particular place in mind, Charles broke up the home in Pueblo and moved his family to Omaha, Nebraska, where they spent one winter. The urge to move stayed with him, although this time the prompting was apparently more *directive* than forceful. Thus, the Fillmores moved to Kansas City, Missouri, in the spring of 1885.

In Kansas City Charles engaged in a form of real-estate speculation called "plunging" and laid out the outline for the Gladstone Heights subdivision. Today several streets still bear the names he gave them, including Myrtle and Norton Avenues, in honor of his wife and his brother. Charles was quite successful at "plunging" until, like the mining boom, the real-estate boom collapsed. Along with countless others, he lost all his material belongings.

Myrtle Fillmore's Healing and Its Influence on Charles

To compound the Fillmores' financial crisis, Myrtle's childhood tubercular illness became complicated by the recurrence of the malaria she had contracted as a young woman.[8] The doctor's prognosis was that she would probably live only a short time. In addition to enduring pain in his short leg and the discomfort of his steel leg brace, Charles began losing sight in his right eye. As a last resort, the Fillmores gave serious consideration to returning to the mountains.

In the spring of 1886, as they contemplated the move, Dr. Eugene B. Weeks, a representative of the Illinois Metaphysical College founded by Emma Curtis Hopkins, arrived in Kansas City. He was scheduled to present a series of lessons on a subject then being referred to as "Christian Science," "New Thought," or "Divine Science."[9] After attending his talks on spiritual healing, Myrtle seized upon the conviction that the source of her life was God and it was not necessary for her to continue suffering the ills of her ancestors. Although it did not come easily, physical improvement began at once, and Myrtle was healed within a year.

News of Myrtle's healing spread so rapidly that soon neighbors and people who lived miles away began requesting her help through healing prayers. Her son, Lowell, later recalled:

Mother seemed always cheerful and helpful, but there came a time when she seemed to grow more cheerful. People from the neighborhood began coming in to see her. She explained to me that she was praying for them. I remember one old gentleman, who lived across the street, came several times using his crutches. Then, one day, I heard Mother tell him to lay down his crutches and walk across the room. He said he couldn't do it, but she insisted that he go ahead and try it. He did try, and walked without his crutches, but it was difficult, for I heard his joints pop. This man was soon healed, as were many others who came in for Mother's help. [10]

At first Charles was too much a practical man to be interested in his wife's newly found involvement with spiritual healing, even though he was in almost constant pain. However, he watched Myrtle's continued success, both with healing herself and with the reported results of answered prayer on behalf of others. Concerning the help she offered, the late Unity historian James Dillet Freeman wrote:

> Like the little leaven that leavens the whole loaf, this thought was to work in her [Myrtle Fillmore] until it had made her every whit whole. It was not to let her go until, through her, thousands had been made whole, too. It was not to let her go until she and her husband, who was soon set afire with it too, had founded a faith that reached around the world and blessed the lives of millions. [11]

Eventually, Charles's interest grew all-consuming and he began to neglect his real-estate business for increased involvement with and promulgation of what his friends deemed a "fanatical delusion." With this "fanatical delusion," Charles's chronic pains ceased, his hip healed and grew stronger, and his leg lengthened until, in a few years, he finally dispensed with the steel extension that he had worn since he was a child.

Emma Curtis Hopkins

The word metaphysics, as used by the growing nineteenth-century New Thought movements, has many definitions. Charles Fillmore called metaphysics "[t]he systematic study of the science of Being; that which transcends the physical. By pure metaphysics is meant a clear understanding of the realm of ideas and their legitimate expression."[12] An influential pioneer in religious metaphysics and the American New Thought movements, Phineas Parkhurst Quimby attracted several significant future teachers in the early 1860s, foremost among them Mary Baker Glover Patterson (later known as Mary Baker Eddy).[13] In 1881 Mrs. Eddy founded Christian Science in Boston. She then abandoned Quimby and in 1883 began publishing the *Christian Science Journal* with the assistance of her student, Emma Curtis Hopkins. The following year, Mrs. Hopkins became the editor of the *Journal*, but was released from that position one year later for reading metaphysical literature other than Mrs. Eddy's writings.[14]

Although she was separated from the Eddy School of Christian Science, Mrs. Hopkins retained what she considered was the best among all her learning experiences, and she remained generous in her attitude toward all Christian Science. In 1887 she wrote:

> Presumptively, if W. S. Adams, who wrote a treatise on Christian Science in 1844, had read Mrs. Eddy's work on Christian Science published about twenty [actually thirty-one] years after his book came out, he would have exclaimed, "Stupendous folly!" He would have been very Christian indeed not to have said so, for he insisted that forced right behavior was Christ's method of training the heart and mind, while she insisted that forced right thinking would train all externals.[15]

Mrs. Hopkins developed the view that each person has a right to his convictions and the fidelity to those beliefs will serve as a "leaven in the midst of flour and water." That is, each individual will experience gratifying continued personal growth.[16]

Emma Curtis Hopkins was unique. She took the theses of "material scientists" and their polar opposites, the "Christian Scientists," Adams, Quimby via Eddy, Mrs. Eddy herself, and her own theses, and from these Mrs. Hopkins produced a synthesis that became the foundation of her eventual teachings. A prolific writer, she founded her own, most influential school. Even the school's original name was an evidence of evolution and synthesis: "Hopkins Metaphysical College." Emma Curtis Hopkins's school attracted numerous students who eventually became teachers of metaphysics and founders of metaphysical movements of their own.

During the course of study with Mrs. Hopkins, the Fillmores became her favorite students and close friends. Later, she often corresponded with them, asking for their assistance with healing prayers for people with whom she was praying.[17] Charles Fillmore expressed his high regard for Mrs. Hopkins through an editorial:

Emma (Curtis) Hopkins will commence a course of lectures on Christian Science at Room 31 Deardorff Building, Kansas City, January 16th, 1890...

Everyone who has a desire to know more of this wonderful philosophy should embrace this opportunity of listening to Mrs. Hopkins. She is undoubtedly the most successful teacher in the world; ... She dwells so continually in the spirit that her very presence heals, and those who listen to her earnest words are filled with new life. These are not the claims of an enthusiast but the carefully sifted testimony of scores of her students. ...

We are not partial to Christian Science as taught by those who are sticklers for many of its dogmas, because in our humble opinion they thresh a whole lot of unnecessary straw in elucidating simple principles. But that they lay hold of an underlying principle, the one great principle that moves the universe — we are satisfied, because we have seen the power demonstrated through them.[18]

Among the several founders of movements and teachers of metaphysics besides Charles and Myrtle Fillmore were Malinda Cramer, the first president of the International Divine Science Association; Helen Williams, the editor of *Wilman's Express*; Ella Wheeler Wilcox, a well-known writer; Annie Rix Militz and Harriet Rix, founders of "Home of Truth" on the West Coast; Mrs. Bingham, teacher of Nona Brooks, founder of the Divine Science movement; and Dr. H. Emilie Cady, who studied with Mrs. Hopkins during a lecture trip to New York City.[19]

The Unity Organization

When ideas evolve to full-scale organizations, it is often difficult to determine when formal organization actually begins. The embryo of the Fillmores' organization, which later became known as Unity School of Christianity, began with their first publication, *Modern Thought*, in 1889;

yet the evolution toward publication began at least three years before. The legal corporation did not become a reality until 1903.

EARLY PUBLICATIONS

In the first issue of *Modern Thought* (April 1889), Charles Fillmore outlined his concept of the magazine's purpose in the religious milieu of the day:

> *Modern Thought* . . . being somewhat of a pioneer in the field, it has to overcome the precedent and prejudice of generations of religious journalism. That a publication devoted to the development of man's spiritual nature could be liberal enough in its ideas to embrace the good in all sects and systems has not heretofore been deemed a possibility.[20]

Charles expressed his conviction that spiritually progressive people desired a close relationship with devotees of all religious persuasions and that such people had grown beyond the creeds, doctrines, and dogmas of denominationalism. The time had arrived, he felt, when words that expressed systems of philosophy and theology would be replaced with words to serve as a yardstick for measuring their value.

As for the magazine's relationship to independent thinking, he clarified:

> It is for the independent Christian, or the independent thinker on any line of spiritual philosophy or science, that *Modern Thought* has a word. . . . Papers and magazines there are by the thousands, the acknowledged exponents of this church and that society, each claiming to point out to man the true path; but where is there one that accords to all its contemporaries the full measure of truth to which they are entitled?

In this vein, he expressed the hope that the existence of *Modern Thought* would be perpetuated by revealing the good in all religions and philosophies and by reminding people that they could serve God without being tied hand and foot to "churchianity." He concluded:

> All these [beliefs and isms] have good within them, and are doing the work needed on their respective planes, but that any church or ism has a copyright on God's truth is preposterous. . . . [W]e have but one standard by which to estimate the truth or error in the

beliefs and creeds of men, and it can be applied successfully to them all —"By their fruits ye shall know them."

The Fillmores' eclectic approach was important to the early success of the Unity publications. After noting that both of the Fillmores had studied Christian Science, New Thought, Quakerism, Theosophy, Rosicrucianism, Spiritism, and Hinduism, although not becoming members of any group, religious researcher Frank Mead concluded: "Out of their studies came an ideology both old and original, built on ancient truths and concepts but moving in new directions."[21]

Considerable evolution occurred during the first three years of publication. One year after its unveiling, the newspaper-format magazine *Modern Thought* became *Christian Science Thought*. A few months later, the name changed to *Thought*, and the magazine assumed a book format. Eleven months later, their second publication, *Unity*, appeared. In October 1895 Charles combined *Thought* and *Unity* into one publication, *Unity*, at first published semimonthly and then monthly. Beyond external changes, the early publications foreshadowed seeds of thought that later grew to be magazines in their own right. For example, in its second month of publication, *Modern Thought* began a "Children's Department." In August 1893 the idea bloomed into *Wee Wisdom*, which became the first children's publication in the United States. Two years later, *Wee Wisdom*, with its "The Youth's Department," planted the seed for the teen magazine that blossomed as *Youth*, first published in January 1927. Later, *Youth* changed to *Progress*, then to *You*, and still later back to *Progress*. In February 1896 an editorial noted the contemplation of *Unity* moving from a monthly publication to a weekly publication. This never happened but eventually a "sister" publication was created in 1909 – *Weekly Unity*.

In 1890 *Modern Thought* introduced a "Bible Study" using the International Bible texts for the current month, published by the International Council of Religious Education, as a basis for metaphysical interpretations. This feature was later carried in other periodicals as well and then in April 1923 a four-page publication appeared under the title *Unity Sunday-School Leaflet*, which presented Bible interpretations.

Daily Word, a monthly magazine of a size for purse and briefcase-carrying convenience, presenting briefly a constructive thought, a short prayer, and a Scripture for each day, first appeared in July 1924. The periodical, which now has a monthly circulation of just over one million, first appeared in embryonic form in *Unity* during the late 1890s.

Born of a desire to make Christian principles practical in the world of commerce, *The Christian Business Man*, later named *Good Business*, was first published in July 1922. Thirty-six years later Hawthorne Books, Inc. published selected *Good Business* articles as an anthology.

Establishment of the Society of Silent Unity

Because the Fillmores believed prayer to be effective, they gathered with friends and neighbors in their home to join in prayer for all those whose needs were known to them. About this embryo prayer ministry, Unity historian Dana Gatlin wrote: "This group, known as the Society of Silent Help, began its ministry in 1890. Besides the Kansas City members, persons in other towns 'sat in' [in their own homes] at the hours of prayer."[22]

The first publication that bore the name *Unity* originally served as the special organ of the Society of Silent Help. During an evening prayer session in the spring 1891, as Charles and Myrtle Fillmore and a few students sat in the silence, the name "Unity" broke into Charles's thoughts, although he had not been thinking about a name just then.

> "That's it!" he [Fillmore] cried out. "'UNITY!' that's the name for our work, the name we've been looking for."
>
> Later he told friends . . . "No one else heard it, but it was as clear to me as though somebody had spoken to me."[23]

Less than a year after the inception of the Society of Silent Help, the Fillmores would change the name to the Society of Silent Unity.

Although praying silently was only occasionally practiced by a few nineteenth-century orthodox Protestant denominations, *silent* prayer was common among nineteenth-century Christian Metaphysicians and mentioned frequently throughout the literature. Although neither Hinduism nor Quakerism is considered to be among Christian Metaphysical movements, both emphasize silence. Since the Fillmores studied both of these religions, we can account for their own emphasis on silence.

The Fillmores wanted to share their learning experiences through silent prayer with their subscribers, as well as with those who lived close by. One method of achieving this sharing was through the addition of a new feature to the magazine, "New Thought." Myrtle was chosen to edit the column and, in announcing the purpose and role of the Society of Silent Help in April 1890, she said the healing experiences already recorded were evidence that physical presence was not required for answered prayer. She further explained:

> [A] little band in this city have agreed to meet in silent soul communion every night at ten o'clock. . . .
>
> Whoever will may join this society, the only requirement being that members shall sit in a quiet, retired place, if possible, at the hour of ten o'clock every night, and hold in *silent thought* for not less than fifteen minutes, the words that shall be given each month by the editor of this department.[24]

The subscribers quickly came to be considered "classes" and their monthly prayer thoughts called "class thoughts." These prayers were of a general nature, to help one in seeking healing, harmonious domestic and business relations, or money. Later, the "class thought" was divided into categories with specific prayers for "healing," "prosperity," and "illumination."

For convenience of the rural community classes, in the second month of its existence the Society of Silent Help changed its class thought or prayer time from 10 P.M. to 9 P.M. This change, which allowed farmers to "sit in" but still retire early enough to arise for early morning chores, was one of the early evidences of Unity's responsiveness to the practical needs of its members.

In May 1890 Myrtle Fillmore wrote: "It should be understood that this department is not intended for trained teachers [of Christian metaphysics], although many of them might be benefited by sitting in the silence each evening, but the object is to start into spiritual unfoldment those who are so situated that they cannot have personal teaching."[25]

The instruction given in the first editorial to "hold silent thought" is in keeping with words and phrases such as *mind, thought, silent, mental, thinking, silent thought, mind power,* and *mental healing,* which abound in the early Unity publications:

> [T]he only effectual cure is that brought about and perfected by Spirit, the real self, through the process of silent thought. . . .

Right thoughts are powerful. . . . It is written in the Bible (KJV), "As a man (*sic*) thinketh in his heart so is he. How necessary then to think right thoughts."[26]

Thought is the vitalizing energy of the world.[27]

In no respect has the philosophy of Mental Healing in its radical form differed more from the original.[28]

[G]ood thoughts are never lost, though they may never be inscribed upon paper, but they are imprinted on our lives, yea, show forth in our bodies, and are read by many.

. . . Even as the children of Israel were kept out of the promised land by what to some might seem trivial errors, so are we keeping ourselves out of our promised land. . . . How many blessings we miss by our careless ways of thinking![29]

Speaking words of prayer is rarely mentioned in the early publications. The phenomena of the *spoken word* concept, that is, prayer given in a specified manner, was left for the Society of Silent Unity to develop in future decades.

DEVELOPMENT OF THE *Spoken Word* CONCEPT

Since Charles and Myrtle Fillmore emphasized the merits of prayer and silence, and since the primary means of communication with the Silent Unity students was their prayer ministry organ, *Unity*, it follows that students were taught "to hold in silent thought," and that "the only effective cure is . . . through the process of silent thought." As the Silent Unity Prayer Ministry grew and became an organization in its own right, its leaders began to encourage speaking the prayer thoughts aloud. In May 1892, *Unity* published a letter to "Each Member of Silent Unity," which stated:

The only difference between you and Jesus is that He had absolute faith that the Father principle would respond to His word. . . .

To show forth . . . health, strength, prosperity, and fullness of joy, you must by your word acknowledge them as yours now. . . . The only object and aim of this society is to get people to place themselves mentally where spirit can suggest the Truth to them, then they must take up these suggestions and incorporate them into their own lives by their *word.* . . .

Those who hold this Jesus Christ ideal constantly before them, and affirm both silently and audibly that what He manifested can be manifested by all, thereby become themselves the Helper.[30]

Sharing most of the Fillmores' ideas was a New York City physician, Dr. H. Emilie Cady, who published a variety of booklets and pamphlets with messages similar to those of the Fillmores. After reading Cady's booklet, "Finding the Christ in Ourselves," Charles solicited her contributions to *Modern Thought* and *Unity.*[31] Dr. Cady accepted the invitation and wrote many articles for the Unity periodicals, several of which were later collected and published as books. One of these books appeared as a series in 1894 and 1895 and was compiled as *Lessons in Truth.* It remains Unity's basic textbook for beginners.[32]

In March 1892 *Unity* published a portion of a letter that Dr. Cady wrote to Myrtle Fillmore as encouragement for her:

Peace, peace, my sister. It is all right. The Master is doing His work through you every moment that you give yourself wholly to Him. "Speak the word only." You are bothering about results because you do not see them. That is His part, not yours. . . . Even when you seem to fail most ignominiously, just say, "that is nothing at all, not worth a moment's notice or regret. Christ in me is still perfect."[33]

In this letter and in other writings, Dr. Cady considerably strengthened the idea of *speaking* words of prayer. In one article, "The Spoken Word," later published as a chapter in *How I Used Truth*, Dr. Cady asserted:

We begin, as God in creation, by speaking out into this formless Substance all about us with faith and power, "Let there be so and so (whatever we want). Let it come forth into manifestation here and now. It does come forth by the power of my word. It is done; it is manifest," and so forth.[34]

The emerging instruction in relation to *speaking* prayer thoughts was a supplement to the *silent thought* approach, not a replacement. The Unity publications indicate that the *spoken word* of prayer is the natural result of holding a thought in mind until an image is established and then completed with an audible expression.

Soon after the Society of Silent Unity began emphasizing the importance of speaking the prayer thought, the concept attained high visibility in Unity publications and in all prayer activities conducted by various departments of Unity School of Christianity. Silent Unity accompanied the instruction to speak constructive words with a warning not to speak destructive words, and with appropriate Scripture in support of the directive:

Woe unto them that decree unrighteous decrees. . . . (Isa. 10:1)

[E]very idle word that men shall speak, they shall give account thereof. . . . For by thy words thou shalt be justified, and by thy words thou shalt be condemned. (Matt. 12:36, 37)

The concept of the *spoken word* aimed at producing unwanted conditions is also clearly based upon Scripture:

Thou shalt decree a thing, and it shall be established unto thee: . . . When men are cast down, then thou shalt say, There is a lifting up. (Job 22:28, 29)

Set a watch, O Lord, before my mouth; keep the door of my lips. (Ps. 119:105)

In the beginning was the Word, and the Word was with God, and the Word was God. The same was in the beginning of God. All things were made by him; and without him was not any thing made that was made. (John 1:1–3)[35]

Therefore I [Jesus] say unto you, what things soever ye desire, when ye pray, *believe* that ye receive them, and ye shall have them [italics added]. (Mark 11:24)

With reference to the *spoken word*, Silent Unity placed special emphasis on the word *believe*. A person needs to conceive him- or herself to be the expression or *pressing out* of God; the student was instructed to believe with the man, Jesus, "I and my Father are one" (John 10:30). Because of what a person conceives him- or herself to be, and because *mind* acts under its own conception of itself, one's word goes from the speaker filled with power to create whatever the speaker says. The prayer of faith stemmed from an unconditional belief in both the ability and the desire of Spirit to hear the call and respond.

Silent Unity taught that when our words are spoken in a consciousness of One Mind or Spirit, then our *spoken word* becomes this life, power, and action. Our words are like molds that indicate in what form our thoughts will be shaped and become a part of the conditions of our life. The word gives form to the unformed, visibility to the invisible, manifestation to the not manifest.

Devotees were asked to decide what they genuinely wished to produce in life *before* speaking. They were told to formulate the idea clearly and then speak the word with authority. Then, having spoken the word, they were to relax, realizing that they had given an order to the subconscious mind, which is said to be entirely responsive to one's conscious thought and one's *spoken word*, whether the word spoken is negative or positive.

Unity students were told that they could build confidence in prayer by daily practicing and experimenting with the *spoken word* and by observing the precision of results. If the words have been constructive, they need not trouble themselves about the results.[36]

Not until 1904 were the written requests for prayer, thousands of which were sent to the Society of Silent Prayer, answered by mail. Since then, all letters, telephone calls, and telegrams have been specifically answered by the Society.[37] In recent years, the Society has added responses to e-mail requests.

In 1904, the Society, now known solely as Silent Unity, began sending prayers along with letters of comfort and instruction. Like the division of "Class Thoughts" in previous publications, these prayers are precisely for needs such as healing, prosperity, guidance, harmony, order, and justice. An instructional pamphlet, "A Manual of Prayer," advises repeating the prayers aloud and/or silently until the request for help is answered.[38] The Silent Unity letters instruct recipients to *declare, state, speak, say*, or *affirm* for themselves, or for whomever they consider in their prayers, the words printed on the leaflet that accompanies the letter. All these instructions are designed to prompt speaking words of prayer aloud with conviction and boldness.

Myrtle Fillmore answered many of those early letters to Silent Unity. Representative extracts from two of her letters, which encourage the petitioner for help, state: "Declare that God's love is being poured out to you from everywhere, and that in it there is no "pity," nothing to weaken or discourage." And "We are rejoicing with you in the overcoming of false states of mind, and declare for you strong words of courage, faith, strength, wisdom, plenty."[39]

The Unity ministry succeeded as its various publications evolved and grew through escalating subscriptions (Unity had 8 employees by 1905 and 350 by 1923).[40] Silent Unity's receipt of mail quickly increased from a few letters daily to several hundred weekly. Myrtle Fillmore was actively involved in all phases of the work, especially her "pet" publication for children, *Wee Wisdom*. Although she continued to work with Silent Unity all her life, in 1916 Myrtle decided to relinquish direction of Silent Unity's activities.

May Rowland, who came to Silent Unity directly from school, received personal training from Myrtle Fillmore, and became director of Silent Unity, a position she held for fifty-five years. After twenty-three years in that position, Mrs. Rowland spoke of Silent Unity's part in the healing process: "The Spirit of God is here with and in us and also with and in those to whom we are ministering. In Spirit there is neither distance nor separation. We speak the word, and the Holy Spirit in the individual does the renewing, healing, restoring work in him."[41]

Another young Silent Unity worker, Frank B. Whitney, headed the Unity Correspondence School beginning in 1916. Whitney became the instrument for developing the long-cherished dream of a publication that would provide a thought, or *word*, for each day. Myrtle Fillmore liked young Whitney's ideas, Charles Fillmore approved, and so in the April 1924 issue of *Unity,* it was announced that a new publication, *Unity Daily Word*, would begin in July 1924 (the name would change to *Daily Word* in 1939). From the beginning, the Fillmores considered *Daily Word* to be written and edited under the inspiration of Silent Unity. However, from 1924 to 1938, F. B. Whitney was listed on the masthead as editor. After Whitney's tenure, following the lead of Silent Unity's impersonal style, *Daily Word* editors were not identified for years, until the mid-1990s. The logotype of the first *Daily Word* cover (July 1924) reads, in part, "Man finds the lost word when he finds within himself his God-given power to create through his word." Each day's exercise includes an affirmative prayer for silent and/or audible use, a brief lesson, and a Scripture, with the selection designed to set the lesson and affirmation in focus.

Two months after its first issue in July 1924, *Daily Word* had 5,300 subscribers.[42] By 1959, James Decker would note: "There are more than a million readers of the English-language edition of *Daily Word*, and it is also published in seven foreign-language editions and in a Braille edition."[43] Since May Rowland was director of the department under whose inspiration *Daily Word* was written and edited, she naturally exerted a strong influence upon the publication. Until her retirement in 1971, she contributed innumerable signed articles and unsigned lessons. Two articles have been reprinted as instruction pamphlets for Silent Unity correspondents: "A Drill in the Silence," and "Come Ye Apart Awhile."[44] In both pamphlets, Mrs. Rowland gives considerable attention to relaxation as preparation for effective prayer.

May Rowland encouraged speaking words of relaxation directly to the various parts of the body, as did her friend and mentor, Myrtle Fillmore. In an article that has been reprinted innumerable times, Myrtle recorded how her own healing was effected:

> [I]t flashed upon me that I might talk to the life in every part of my body and have it do just what I wanted . . .
>
> I told the life in my liver that it was not torpid or inert, but full of vigor and energy. I told the life in my stomach that it was not weak or inefficient, but energetic, strong, and intelligent . . .
>
> I went to all the life centers in my body and spoke words of Truth to them—words of strength and power.[45]

In discussing the increasing use of the spoken word, Charles Fillmore wrote in "Heal the Sick," now a Silent Unity pamphlet: "Speak the first word of Truth that comes to you. Speak it silently until you have courage to speak it aloud; but don't fail to speak it. Silent words do their work, but audible words, rightly said, bring quicker results."[46]

Mrs. Rowland explained why audible words bring quicker results. She said that the words one speaks exist and move through a universe of vibration and energy that take form just as one shall decree. Because they are formative expressions of what is thought, those words literally "mold" one's life.[47]

Unlike many writers on the *spoken word* concept, Mrs. Rowland encouraged speaking aloud the word-idea one wishes to see manifest, and then writing it out as well. She said, "This helps to establish in your consciousness exactly what you want . . . put it . . . some place where you can forget the problem for the moment and let your word work."[48]

Mrs. Rowland and Silent Unity also followed the Fillmores' lead by warning that times of prayer are *not* for begging or beseeching God. Simultaneously, they remind us that through thought and word, prayer *is* the vehicle for identifying with Infinite Mind, one of the names Unity calls God.

For all the prayer efforts of Silent Unity on behalf of those who write to them, they receive, and have since 1890, countless letters attesting to the effectiveness of the spoken words or affirmations which the letter writers have received from Silent Unity. With written authorization, selected testimonial letters have appeared in print from the second issue of *Unity* to the present and later in the other Unity periodicals as well. Periodically, a booklet of testimonials is compiled for mailing to correspondents, as additional encouragement in prayer.[49]

The Unity publications, the Silent Unity Prayer Ministry, and Silent-70 (the department that sends free literature to thousands of institutions and individuals in need) all met with phenomenal success. The message spread rapidly, first around the Kansas City area, then across the United States, and then, via the printed word, into many other countries. The movement grew through a ministerial education program and the establishing and expansion of Unity study groups and churches throughout the world. In addition, many people have taken advantage of the adult curriculum that is provided annually through a continuing education program and a variety of spiritual retreats.

Spreading the Unity Teaching

The Fillmores gave high priority to instructing Unity students in metaphysical principles. In the early years, their teaching was directed at adults being introduced to Christian metaphysics for the first time, but Charles and Myrtle continued to seek ways to reach people outside the

Kansas City area who were interested in Unity teaching and healing work.[50]

By 1916 many recipients of the printed word began requesting local classes. The first step was mimeographing some of Charles Fillmore's lessons, thereby establishing a correspondence school with courses similar in content to the primary courses the Fillmores taught in Kansas City. Courses were presented in a series of twelve lessons, with students receiving one lesson at a time. Students studied the material, then answered the questions on the lesson from the school. Students would then return their answers to Unity headquarters for grading and response from the Fillmores. Within two years from its inception, the correspondence school had more than 2,000 enrollees.[51]

Despite this success, requests for local classes persisted. Many Unity students who completed the correspondence course, attended classes in Kansas City, and read Unity literature sought to establish centers of Unity work in their local communities. In 1915 Unity School decided to support these efforts by establishing a "Field Department" within Unity School. The Field Department saw its mission as "assisting in organizing study classes and centers among groups of students who are interested in applying the Jesus Christ principles in their lives and in their affairs." The purpose of the work was "to encourage cooperation, harmony and constructive methods in the advancement of Truth."[52]

The study-class idea caught on. The steps for organizing such classes were simple. An interested person would make arrangements for a place to hold an opening meeting, usually in someone's home, and notify Unity a few weeks in advance. Unity would then notify their readers of the time and location of the meeting, and the class would begin. The Fillmores continued their emphasis on study classes and centers as opposed to churches and ministries. They felt that although Unity presented a spiritual teaching in the field of religion, the work was not a sect or a church.

The logical next step would have been to establish a course of instruction at Unity School for the licensing of Unity teachers, and to set up a training school for ordaining ministers. Charles and Myrtle Fillmore wished to avoid making Unity a denomination and, therefore, resisted both of these moves. They were concerned that "ministers" and "services" would clash with the message of complete personal freedom in worship. The Fillmores wanted to develop a fellowship of students who would take their new understanding back to their churches for sharing and so avoided proselytizing. They sought no converts and made no missionary efforts.[53] After noting the structural change from a religious publishing house and a loosely knit prayer ministry to an organization with licensed teachers and ordained ministers, religious researcher Marcus Bach forecast: "There is no reason to believe that the Unity School of Christianity will not one day be rated as a denomination. The pattern is already becoming apparent. Some eighty years young, it is already a church of striking proportions."[54]

At first, leaders of local groups called their organizations fellowships, associations, study groups, and centers, primarily in an effort to avoid using the word *church*. Today, although names of local groups still vary greatly, the field activities in the United States and abroad are coordinated by a self-governing organization, the Association of Unity Churches, International. (Administrative offices are located in Lee's Summit, Missouri, three miles from Unity Village.)

Following Charles Fillmore's example, Unity ministers and licensed teachers encourage students to establish and maintain direct, personal communication with God and not to depend upon secondary sources, not even the Unity leaders themselves. Like Fillmore before them, today's Unity leaders attempt to provide their students with the tool of the *spoken word* (see pp. 14-17), and with the tool of Scriptural interpretation that relates to the student's everyday life and needs. To this concern, we now turn.

Among Orthodox Christian views of the Bible, one discovers that the Catholic, Lutheran, Episcopal, Anglican, and Reformed Churches are in similar streams of thought. Each views the Bible as the clear, perfect, inspired, and authoritative word of God and guide of man.[55] The fundamentalists, including Baptists, Nazarenes, and Pentecostals, hold views of the Bible similar to the group previously discussed. However, this second group adds the *doctrinal* insistence that the individual conscience must be the interpreter of the Bible.[56] In practice, this means that the individual conscience can be relied upon as the absolute interpreter of the Bible, so long as the conscience perceives in harmony with the fundamentalist's *doctrinal* perspectives. These include Scripture-based statements of belief, with such particular emphasis on *certain* Scripture as to make them appear inordinately important in relation to the rest of the

Bible, for example, the ordinances of Baptism and of Holy Communion, based upon the Last Supper.

Most liberal churches do not believe that the Bible is infallible, or that the books of the Bible are of equal value and importance. This free-spirited branch of Protestantism, particularly Unitarianism, and Universalism (since May 1961 the Unitarian Universalist Association) tend to place emphasis upon those portions of Scripture that appear to endorse social action and political reform.[57]

The New Thought branch of the Christian tree, the Unity movement in particular, considers the Bible an important book of inspiration and guidance. However, they teach that not all of the Bible can be accepted literally and that it must be interpreted practically and inspirationally. Their method is, therefore, called metaphysical interpretation.

Charles Fillmore's Metaphysical Interpretation of Biblical Literature

Since Charles Fillmore was an eclectic, he studied the Scriptures of varied cultures and the doctrines of the *isms* that grew in relationship to those Scriptures. But he was not satisfied with studying what others said about the great prophets or teachers—particularly Jesus. He closely studied the words *of* Jesus and not just the words *about* Him, a process that inspired Charles Fillmore to conclude that all religious experience could be firsthand and personal. This conclusion led him to teach that no person needed an intermediary between himself/herself and God.

To aid his students in their search for meaning in Christian Scriptures, Fillmore published a commentary on the International Sunday School Bible Lessons in the earliest Unity periodicals. Finally, in 1931, Fillmore completed the monumental task of compiling his commentaries and publishing the *Metaphysical Bible Dictionary*, with considerable assistance from Theodosia DeWitt Schobert and with historical and etymological research by Paul M. Rigby.[58]

The *Dictionary* is a scholarly work, offering first the correct pronunciation and then the Hebrew, Aramaic, or Greek definition of the name of the person, town, river, place, sea, or thing described, plus clarification of significant words and phrases, and, finally, their esoteric meanings. The *Dictionary*'s preface explains that great care has been exercised in the compilation of word definitions after consulting with numerous authorities and lexicons. Wherever the etymology has not become lost, the definitions have been traced back to their origins.

Max Dessoir called for this type of research in 1906: "Only the very beginning of a word's life are like a glimpse of sunlight. Then the word is still fresh and vigorous, not faded or worn out; its whole meaning is grasped by everyone. From this insight poets have returned to the original meanings of words, to rough dialectical forms and natural metaphors." That "glimpse of sunlight" was one of Fillmore's aims. He taught that understanding the meaning of proper names in the Bible is as essential to a suitable interpretation of the Bible as, in the words of one of his students, "a knowledge of numerical values is to solving mathematical problems."[59]

Fillmore believed that in reading the Bible silently or aloud, and praying about its inner meaning, the student could successfully interpret Scripture for him- or herself. The man who succeeded Fillmore as minister of the Unity Society of Practical Christianity in 1933, the late Dr. Ernest C. Wilson, shared with me:

> His [Fillmore's] Bible classes were workshops where he sometimes worked out interpretations which were later published. However, the usual order of presentation reversed: he would read a Scriptural lesson aloud and then read his handwritten, if not published, interpretation to the class in order to launch discussion. Charles never claimed a *divine* revelation which was not available to all, but submitted his understanding of the Bible lesson to the class for their evaluation and judgment.[60]

Fillmore felt that the students' experiences would help to determine the specifics of interpretation, thereby making their understanding personal and practical, as well as universal.

Fillmore offers a definition in the *Dictionary*'s preface: "By the term 'metaphysical' we refer to the inner or esoteric meaning of the name defined, as it applies to every unfolding individual and to his relation to God."[61] Fillmore declared that he received an understanding of what the characters of Scripture *represented* (not etymological definitions of names) by opening his mind to completely new revelations and interpretations. In a 1939 interview he told Dana Gatlin:

Meditating on the inner meaning of the life of Jesus Christ, we find and gradually realize that it is much more than a mere history. It is an account of unfoldment—a revelation of spiritual principles—that is being perpetually carried on and evidenced in all life everywhere. Gradually we perceive and understand and realize these eternal principles.[62]

A metaphysical or spiritual interpretation of biblical literature regards its allegorical nature as of primary importance. Unity believes that if Scripture is intended for the enlightenment of humankind and the development of the spiritual nature, the Scripture must have a special significance of which historical narrative is the obvious part. Studying the Bible with this view in mind opens additional avenues of personal enrichment.

However, many think that to say that there are portions of the Bible not intended to be accepted literally is to blaspheme. Not all of those who read or listen to a reading of a Unity interpretation of Scripture are favorably impressed. On this account, Unity has many critics. Harold Berry observes: "Because of Unity's allegorical interpretation of the Bible, they have twisted obvious truths and made them teach something entirely different."[63]

On the other hand, an important viewpoint that supports Charles Fillmore's right to, and method of, personal interpretation is expressed in the *Encyclopedia of Religion and Ethics*:

It is not easy to give a quite satisfactory definition of metaphysics. The name throws no real light upon its nature, having referred originally merely to the order of some Aristotelian treatises. . . . For the purpose of this sketch, . . . [i]t will be convenient to divide the treatment of it into three parts: (1) the general nature of knowledge, (2) the conception of reality and its chief applications, and (3) the bearings of metaphysics on other subjects, especially ethics and religion. . . .

(g) Religion. A chief element in the higher forms of religion consists in a certain intensification of the moral consciousness . . . combined with the conviction that the object of ultimate valuation is real and attainable. A conviction of this kind is sometimes based rather on some *form of intuition or of revelation* or on the authority of some great teacher, or simply on the intrinsic force of the moral principle itself. The founders of the religions and their most influential prophets have generally connected their teaching with some doctrines of a more or less explicitly metaphysical character. Buddhism . . . seems to be rather intimately connected with those Indian forms of metaphysical construction that had their origin in the *Upanishads* [*sic*]. . . . Christianity was perhaps in its origin less definitely metaphysical; but it has been to a large extent interpreted, in the course of its historical development, by means of Platonic and more or less kindred conceptions, and in some of its more recent phases is hardly distinguishable from the more esoteric forms of Buddhism.

. . . [O]n the whole, none of the deeper forms either of metaphysical construction or of religious insight has represented the ideal [moral] as attainable in any other way than *through the individual choice of what is best*.[64]

Fillmore's method of interpretation is a "form of intuition or of revelation"; expressed in his words, it is "a revelation of spiritual principles." His insistence that all people can read the Scriptures aloud or silently, meditate upon them, and metaphysically interpret for themselves is another way of saying that moral ideas are attained, as suggested above, "through the individual choice of what is best." Again, Fillmore's successor, Wilson, told me:

I think Mr. Fillmore felt his ideas were inspired but they were gleaned from many sources, Yoga, C.S. [Christian Science], Spiritualism, Theosophy, etc., as well as from his own subconscious. He always reserved the right to change his mind about his teaching. Certainly there are tenable interpretations besides those he gave. He would be the first to admit this.[65]

Fillmore explained that the purpose of the *Metaphysical Bible Dictionary* is to equip the student of metaphysics with a condensed version of "hidden mysteries," to prompt the student to further self-exploration and new personal discoveries for use amid the inconstancies of everyday life. He considered the *Dictionary* an epitome of the entire Unity viewpoint and teaching, concerned with the Bible, not just as history, but with the inner interpretation of both Testaments.[66] This metaphysical approach is akin to the intuitive concept of oral interpretation as advocated by Hiram Corson.[67]

Although Fillmore accepted the Bible's worth as a historical document, he felt that needless debate centered around trying to prove its historical accuracy and authorship. He cherished the idea that what was really important was that the books of the Bible contain a message for the ages. A brief yet complete example of a scriptural message is extracted from Fillmore's *Mysteries of Genesis:*

> Gen. 3:21. And Jehovah God made for Adam and for his wife coats of skins, and clothed them. (ASV)
>
> Man originally was connected with the warm currents of spiritual life, but when these currents were broken by thought of separation, he required protection from external invading thoughts, hence the "coat of skins." This need is evidenced by the outer skin covering the nerves of our body and the danger of infection when this covering is broken. When a spiritual thought becomes supreme in consciousness the "coat of skins" gives way to the manifestation of the spiritual body broken by Paul. Corruptible flesh is the manifestation of corrupt ideas in mind. "Be ye transformed [changed from] by the renewing of your mind."[68]

Fillmore taught that the Bible represents humankind's spiritual evolution, not from beginning to end, but from within each story a particular phase of familiar life is revealed. The Bible relates humankind's progression for a while and then its retrogression, all evolving toward the highest mental, moral, and spiritual thinking represented in Scripture by the man Jesus.

Although Bible scholars have authenticated many Bible stories as factual, a Bible story is not *just* an incident that occurred thousands of years ago. It is symbolic of an occurrence that takes place within each person who is presently on the path of spiritual progress and evolution. Hence, every phase of religious experience appears in the Bible, so that each person sees a reflection of his or her own character in its varied expressions within the Bible.

Charles R. Fillmore, grandson of the Fillmores and former president of Unity School, has the following to say about the Bible as a record of everyday experience:

Unity is an adventure because it makes our Holy Bible come vividly
alive for us. . . . The seemingly historical actions described in the
Bible are going on in you and in me and in every other human being
this very instant!

. . . Jesus Christ, the greatest character in the Bible, represents
man's greatest characteristic, his spiritual nature. Every place in
the Bible represents a state of mind, and every event represents a
process now in operation in each of us here, today.[69]

Unity teaches that the Bible is not only more inspirational when its
esoteric or metaphysical meaning is sought, but its practical assistance to
the followers of the man, Jesus, is greatly increased. The "letter" of the
Bible, either as history or as an advocate of ritualism, does the student of
Scripture little good. The interpretation, as it pertains to individual
unfoldment or "spirit" of the Bible, is the vital essence of the Truth the
Bible teaches. As with other Unity theories, it is suggested that the student study with an open mind, accept what can be used immediately, and
then set the balance aside for later evaluation.[70]

An Overview

Unity School of Christianity and the Unity Society of Practical Christianity in Kansas City are distinct organizations, and have been since the turn
of the twentieth century. Unity School is the larger organization,
embodying numerous departments to minister to the spiritual needs of
people worldwide. The society serves as one of the local Unity ministries, housed in a church-like structure in Kansas City, and is called
"Unity Temple on the Plaza."

There is also a distinction between Fillmore, cofounder and president
of Unity School of Christianity, and Fillmore, minister of the local congregation in Kansas City. In the former capacity, he had a strong influence, both through his belief in the power of the spoken word and in his
method of interpreting Scripture. Through the printed word, Fillmore
influenced the lives of people around the world and, at home, through
training classes. He also influenced the professional lives of the licensed
teachers and ordained ministers whom he taught personally. In the latter capacity, he was the minister from 1889 to 1933.

Although he retired as local minister in 1933, Fillmore remained president of Unity School of Christianity until his death in 1948. During the fifteen years from his retirement until his death, Fillmore continued researching, writing, field lecturing, and lecturing in summer school sessions at Unity School.

Thus far, this chapter has been concerned primarily with two teaching devices developed by Charles Fillmore and his coworkers: the concept of the spoken word, and metaphysical interpretation of the Bible. The metaphysical interpretation seems to be closely related to the intuitive concepts of reading aloud favored, as stated above, by such writers as Hiram Corson, as well as by some oral interpretation of teachers today.

In keeping with the Fillmore/Unity viewpoint, I emphasize that the nature of the questions one asks *of* and *about* the Bible, as well as questions about the power of the *spoken word*, determines the nature of the answers one receives. Therefore, to receive *appropriate*, not to say *right*, answers, one must ask *appropriate* questions about the power of the *spoken word* and about personal understanding through biblical interpretation. Fillmore/Unity systems and theories are indispensable to the Unity student, ordering thought and allowing the devotee to determine for him- or herself what he or she believes.

Religious teachers and prophets have always prayed and admonished their students to do likewise, but not all have taught a specific prayer method designed to effect tangible results such as healing, prosperity, harmony, and guidance. Fillmore was unique in teaching such a method. Through the ongoing service of the Silent Unity Prayer Ministry and its spoken word tradition of prayer, Unity continues to uplift the lives of those who contact the prayer ministry via mail, telegrams, e-mail, telephone, and in person, for help through prayer. Currently, Silent Unity averages 2.3 million prayer requests per year.[71]

Since the earliest oral tradition of scriptural literature became written literature, non-Christians and Christians alike have sought to interpret and understand what has been written. Further studies of ways to interpret Scripture other than metaphysically, for example, exegetically and hermeneutically, are in order.[72] So long as there are sacred writings and so long as there are people with an inherently religious nature, these studies will be made.

Unlike many religious leaders of his day, Fillmore believed that an *appropriate* understanding of and belief in Scripture did not preclude embracing scientific research. He gave an address, "Unity of Religion and Science," at a meeting of the World Fellowship of Faiths in conjunction with the Century of Progress Exposition in Chicago in 1933. Fillmore anticipated a harmony between religion and science ultimately, and he laid major foundation stones for creating a bridge between the two:

> . . . the proved facts of scientific research and discovery have bit by bit broken down the wall of narrow dogmatic assumptions reared by Christianity, and we are finding that we have, like the Pharisees of Jesus' time, been making the dead letter of Scripture revelation take the place of the living Christ.[73]

Fillmore did not rest on static, unchanging doctrine, and through his system of interpretation, he showed that the spirit of Scripture itself, in fact, was dynamically alive.

Scientists experimenting with the power of the spoken word in recent decades are attempting to show a relationship, not just to the human body, but to flowers, vegetables, and other plant life by speaking words such as *hate* and *love*. In the mid-1970s scientist Lawrence Pinneo designed a computer to read the human mind. In a report, after several experiments with his brainchild's ability to detect the effect of speaking words silently or audibly, Pinneo, who was director of neurophysiology research at Stanford, said that "the mind-reading machine does better at recognizing a spoken word than a silent thought."[74]

When exploring possibilities and the question is asked, "How can we better serve humankind in the future?" it is important to recognize that we need both religious and scientific studies. In particular, quantitative analyses of the spoken word phenomenon as it relates to memory patterns of humanity and to the suggestibility of animate and inanimate entities can provide provocative information.

Fillmore taught that Jesus' message was a living message. Fillmore's students and teachers are determined to maintain that "living" quality about Jesus' message by insisting, as Fillmore himself did, that even while accepting instruction as to methods of interpretation, each student must interpret Scripture for himself/herself. Several other early New Thought leaders, like Ernest Holmes, for example, also encouraged individual and prayerful study of the Scriptures and practicing Truth principles in one's daily living.

Like the Unity teachings themselves, I offer no final solutions. Unity attempts to point students to methods for receiving their own solutions and to encourage continuing unfoldment, not to spoonfeed beliefs or solutions handed down from "on high" by a clerical hierarchy. Unity does not claim to be an easy religion to follow. In fact, with its insistence on self-discipline to induce personal growth, Unity is one of the most demanding regimens of spiritual unfoldment.

With spiritual unfoldment as their purpose, Unity students, teachers, and ministers are resolute that the Unity message will not atrophy by becoming a monument either to the man Jesus, or to the man Charles, or to the woman Myrtle. Unity teachers and ministers today, like their mentor, Charles Fillmore, issue an ongoing invitation to self-exploration through all the systems and theories that they teach. The Unity leaders place considerable emphasis on the power that is humankind's through the ability to change one's personal world through the spoken word and to better understand one's self and one's fellow humankind through reinterpreting Scripture for one's self.

The Unity Student and the Pursuit of Health: Spirit, Mind, Body 2

Mental Health Professionals and the Unity Student

U NITY PEOPLE are eclectic in their pursuit of spirituality as well as in their pursuit of spiritual and psychological health.[1] While no two Unity students necessarily describe their spiritual experiences or beliefs in exact, and at times not even under similar terms, what academic and clinical psychiatrists, psychologists, and other mental health professionals need to know about treating mental health problems in persons with a Unity background is that nearly all hold one belief in common: That all persons are triune beings (spirit, mind, body).

In addressing the mental health problems of a Unity student (as most prefer to be called), a mental health care professional needs to address all three areas of the student's being. Most Unity students increasingly consider it a "given" that a therapist will explore the effects their distress is having on the three phases of their person: spirit, mind, body.[2] (Unity students do not use "and" before the third word in the series precisely because they do not believe one can effectively separate the three: they are "one.")

Because of Unity students' belief that they are one—spirit, mind, body—they feel a pervasive sense that even their "chaotic" experiences will ultimately be resolved. Increasingly, those with mental/emotional problems recognize that they are in the midst of personal change and transition that may even take on the guise of an overwhelming turbulence. At times they express the feeling that their world as they have come to know it is coming to an end—an awe-inspiring and a fearsome experience. They may experience terrible anxiety and at the same time feel hopeful, believing they have come to an important crossroad in their ongoing spiritual development. They see, sometimes in a painful way and at other times with simple, painless clarity, that their present turmoil is part of their evolution into the next phase of personal and spiritual growth, which may well include an expanded awareness that they are a spirit, mind, body. This sense of an ultimately optimistic outcome and the desire to experience it substantially guides the Unity person in the selection of a mental health professional.

Treatments and Medications

Whatever the phase of being requiring specific attention (i.e., spirit, mind, body), a majority of Unity students tend not to take over-the-counter or prescription medication. Exceptions might include short-term use of analgesics for pain relief or antibiotics to treat infection. There are three basic reasons for this consistent behavior among Unity people:

1. They have an inherent belief, underscored by their spiritual studies, that spontaneous healing is possible and have a vested interest in not over providing external help.
2. They are inclined to look to other modalities of treatment besides, or in addition to, medication.
3. They wish to play an active role in their treatment.

A Harvard Medical School (1993) survey indicated that 20 percent of the general population with depression turns to alternative therapies, suggesting that these persons wanted to play an active role in their treatment.[3] In a similar survey of Unity students (Unity ministers, licensed teachers, and laity), 87 percent reported that they actively participated in their own treatment whether working with a spiritual counselor, a physical or a mental health care professional.[4] Furthermore, 81 percent sought alternative therapies either instead of or concurrent with traditional mental health care.

The 87 percent of students reported previously indicated that two major roles they played in their own mental, physical, or spiritual health care were (a) the category of health care professional they chose and (b) who they chose to work with as a health care professional. Eighty percent reported they prayed for guidance about both (a) and (b). They hold sacred their individual right to such selection, much as advocated by psychiatrist John M. Dorsey:

I cannot imagine what it would be like to be unable to choose my own physician, but I cherish that freedom of choice quite as I cherish my civic right to choose the religious living which I prefer. I consider "taking a physician" to be almost as private and personal a matter as "taking a mate." Where my health is concerned I need as much harmony of spirit, consent of will, and unification of self-consciousness as I can mobilize, in order to recover and maintain my clear sense of the wholeness-allness-unity of my human being. Thus, I might not choose you, on account of your extreme subjectivist theories, but if anyone else wished to choose you, I hold that he should not be denied that possibility.[5]

Having made the choice of health care professional(s), Unity students also report that they actively take part in the decision making regarding the type of treatment they will participate in, whether mental, physical, or spiritual. These people have an expressed interest in moving from disease management to promotion of both their own and others' health by incorporating the principles of integrative medical treatment.

Evolution of Medical Terms in the Thinking of Unity Students

The use of the term *integrative medical treatment* is evidence of evolution in the thinking of the Unity student. Unity people were among the first to adopt the use of the term *alternative medicine,* some as long ago as the late 1950s. Typically, all modalities of treatment which were not allopathic medicine were placed in the "alternative" category, with other modalities in their own groupings, for example, chiropractors, nutritionists, and herbalists. Some students began to recognize that the word *alternative* connoted an "either/or" rather than a "both/and" range of options, which seemed to be a threat to both the patient and physicians, and began using the term *complementary medicine* during the mid 1980s, as did some members of the allopathic medical profession.

Later, in the early 1990s, Unity people began adopting the term *integrative medicine* and recently have begun using the terms *integrative modalities of treatment* or *integrative medical treatment* interchangeably with *integrative medicine.*

Unity students believe that God indwells humankind and all creation and that prayer and meditation are the direct access routes to an awareness of that indwelling Presence. Over 80 percent of Unity people do not think of treatments by chiropractors, use of nutritional supplements for physical and emotional problems, high-performance eating plans, acupuncture, prayer and meditation, therapeutic touch, healing hover touch, osteopathy, vitamin and mineral therapy, breathing exercises, etc., as peripheral to general medicine but rather as a part of the core of integrative modalities of treatment. The Unity student sees the various disciplines of health care as being part of the entrée with allopathy and not as incidental side dishes.

As noted earlier, Unity students are eclectic in many ways, including their pursuit of mental and physical health and well-being. They tend to read, study, and experiment with myriad ways to maintain health and to regain health for any of the three phases of being—spirit, mind, body— once it has broken down. Eighty percent of those who responded to the Association of Unity Churches survey exercise from one to six times a week, from fifteen to forty-five minutes each time. Even those who do not exercise regularly know of the benefits of exercise.

Exercises and spiritual practices with a physical component that are most often engaged in by adult Unity students are tai chi, hatha yoga, martial arts, stair climbing, golf, brisk walking, swimming, dance, low-impact aerobics, hiking, bicycling, and stretching. They generally practice, or at least have read about or studied, relaxation techniques, meditation, nutrition, breathing exercises, etc. Many of these studies are included in the adult education programs of the ministry they attend.[6] The study and practice of *pranayama*, a part of the ancient East Indian breath control associated with yoga, is a popular class in the Unity adult education classroom. Pranayama is both authentic spiritual practice and one of the pathways to regaining and maintaining mental and physical health. A mental health practitioner who would work well with a Unity patient/client might prescribe a varying combination of the previously discussed practices.

The Need to Treat the Whole Person

In order to treat mental health problems in a person with a Unity background, the mental health caregiver needs to treat the whole person—

spirit, mind, body. In their eclectic pursuit of complex interests, Unity students are likely to have learned of the side effects of the three types of prescription antidepressants, tricyclics, monamine oxidase inhibitors, and serotonin reuptake inhibitors (especially Prozac). If depression is only mild to moderate in severity, the therapist might wish to avoid these drugs and consider with the patient important lifestyle choices and/or herbal medication alternatives, such as St. John's wort extract. Andrew Weil observes:

> St. John's wort . . . used in Europe for 15 years (prescriptions in Germany now outnumber those for Prozac 25 to 1) . . . was until recently largely dismissed by our own medical community. . . . Meanwhile, a major multi-center trial of the herb is finally in the works here, involving the National Institute of Mental Health (NIMH) and the National Institutes of Health's Office of Alternative Medicine.[7]

Unity students might also choose other natural products, including passion flower, kava extract, oat straw, valerian, amino acid therapy, or ginkgo biloba extract, which are purported to offer antidepressant effects.

Seasonal affective disorder (commonly known as "cabin fever" in northeastern Ohio and southeastern Michigan, locations of my last two churches before becoming CEO in our international offices) has a number of useful home remedies known to many Unity students who live in those somewhat damp and cloudy climates. These home remedies might also be prescribed by a mental health care professional. In addition to taking nutritional and herbal antidepressants instead of, or in addition to, seeking assistance from a mental health care professional, Unity students may include in their regimen of self-care—or respond well to the health care professional's suggestions—to plan a winter vacation in a sunny climate if at all possible; remove or trim from around windows vegetation and/or open shades and blinds which prevent sunlight from entering through windows; receive a massage from a professional masso-therapist if possible or from a friend or family member if necessary; and exercise outdoors at midday, every day if possible. Finally, a popular home remedy in treatment of seasonal affective disorder, which is also used by both alternative and conventional medicine, is to sit in front of a fluorescent light that is ten to twelve times brighter than average indoor light for two hours daily.

The "Talking Cure" and Nutritional Therapy

The Unity student may be willing to continue talking with the trained therapist but would welcome other treatment programs that address the needs of spirit, mind, body. For example, as an option to drugs to correct the brain's chemical imbalances, which may trigger clinical depression, the Unity person generally prefers nutritional therapy, which may reestablish a healthy balance of brain chemicals through less powerful medicines. As suggested in the work of Althoff, Williams, Molvig, and Schuster, "The amino acid tryptophan is needed for the synthesis of serotonin, a mood-regulating norepinephrine."[8] If they are lacking, adding these amino acids is one way that will help to regain balance of brain chemicals.

Before pursuing these subjects further, I must state for the benefit of the nonprofessional reader/prospective Unity patient who has not already studied and discovered options to psychoactive drugs with possible undesired side effects that one needs to exercise caution regarding self-diagnosis. While it is useful to "listen" to your body, mind, spirit and to determine needs and courses of action, it cannot be overemphasized that it is also good to work with a health care professional regarding the use of nutritional products. If you are already using a prescribed medicine such as either one of the benzodiazepines (Valium and Xanax are two of the better known versions) or Prozac, mentioned previously, you must work closely with your physician before discontinuing any drug.[9] One should also not mix herbal extracts with other psychoactive drugs. If you wish to consider more natural methods, be certain to discuss it with your therapist. Should the physician need more information about the integrative modalities of treatment, this can be found in the studies referenced in this chapter (studies published in medical journals and other health care publications).

Diets Popular with Unity Students

Unity people generally attempt to be well informed about nutrition. They consider their diet as important to mental health as it is to physical health; their four basic diets are (a) a vegetarian diet (no animal foods or animal by-products), (b) a lacto-ovo vegetarian diet (dairy products as the only animal foods), (c) a general diet that includes as meats only fish with scales and poultry (skinned), and (d) a general diet that includes moderate amounts of red meat. Of those Unity students responding to the Association of Unity Churches, International survey, 47 percent report following one of the first three diets.

There are also specific diets for persons with different blood types (e.g., type A and O).[10] With regard to the effects of diet on my own health in relationship to my blood type (type A), I relate the following experience. After years of eating very little red meat, I "decided" to add much more red meat, at least three or four times per week. After nine months of that, my energy level greatly reduced. My usually high energy level returned after I discontinued red meat altogether. Diets of Unity students are often rounded out with nutritional supplements, easily available from health food stores, for both physical and mental problems.

A number of researchers suggest a relationship between blood sugar and human behavior. For example, a well-dressed woman visited internist Dr. Marc Siegel without an appointment.[11] She said that she was diabetic. Upon checking, Dr. Siegel determined that the diabetes was controlled. Over several weeks, Dr. Siegel recognized that there seemed to be a relationship between radically different glucose levels and radical changes among the various emerging personalities of the woman who now appeared to have dissociative identity disorder. Dr. Marc Siegel referred the woman to psychiatrist Dr. Greg Alsip. Concerned for her safety, Dr. Alsip placed her in a New York City hospital.

The nurses quickly noticed that the glucose level of each personality was different from each of the other personalities. At a glucose level of 80, the patient expressed a male personality who wondered why he had been referred to a psychiatrist. One of the female personalities with extremely erratic behavior had a glucose level of 250. Some of the personalities tended to be diabetic. Others clearly were not diabetic. While

Dr. Alsip was able to draw this patient back to the most stable personality, that of the woman with controlled diabetes, he appropriately did not draw conclusions based on this one case.

It would be most difficult to determine whether a dangerously high blood sugar level caused extraordinarily erratic behavior or whether the extraordinarily erratic behavior prompted the dangerously high blood sugar level. The causative relationship probably would not be possible to determine with a single case study, although it is suggestive.

A Unity student who was aware of the possible correlation of blood sugar to behavior might well feel comforted if a psychiatrist or other mental health care professional ordered a blood sugar test and then took the results into consideration while planning and providing a treatment program.

The Impact of Spiritual Practice on Mental and Physical Health

The late researcher, psychiatrist, and president of the National Institute for Healthcare Research, David Larson, stated, "Not only is religious commitment associated with improved coping and recovery from both physical and mental illness, but a number of recent studies have suggested that religious commitment could also have a prophylactic or preventative effect on physical and mental health."[12]

The following statement follows Larson's previous observation concerning research into the factors of faith and prayer: "Of 300 studies on spirituality in scientific journals, the National Institute for Healthcare Research found nearly three-fourths showed that religion had a positive effect on health. Research also shows four out of five patients want doctors to ask them about their faith, and one in two want their doctors to pray with them."[13] Despite this, according to a *USA Today* survey, only 10 percent of people indicated that their doctors had "talked to them about their faith as a factor in their healing."

The Association of Unity Churches, International survey supports Larson's position, and in the case of Unity people, the data goes slightly beyond his conclusions regarding the desire to discuss their faith and considerably beyond regarding their desire for prayer. Eighty-two percent said that it was "important" to "very important" that their health care professional have an understanding of the impact of the spiritual realm on their health, mental and physical.

Regarding their choice of mental health care professional, the Association of Unity Churches, International survey asked respondents to check as many as applied to them (totaling more than 100 percent) and to indicate whom they would go to first for assistance. Of the three considered to be mental health professionals by Unity people, 78 percent of Unity students (all three categories, i.e., ministers, licensed teachers, and laity shared this percentage almost exactly) would go first to a spiritual counselor, 41 percent would either go first to a psychologist or to a psychologist in addition to a spiritual counselor, and 17 percent would either go first to a psychiatrist or to a psychiatrist in addition to a spiritual counselor.

The first choice, to seek help from a spiritual counselor, is made specifically because the Unity student knows that he or she will be prayed with during the course of a consultation. Among the same survey respondents, 53 percent would agree to the use of herbal/natural medicines, 25 percent would agree to prescription medicine, 9 percent would agree to over-the-counter medications, and the balance would not take medicine. According to David Larson:

> Most doctors ignore the fact that their patients are fans of God and
> . . . that 60 percent of the population would like to discuss spiritual
> issues with their doctors and 40 percent would like their doctors
> to pray with them . . . Neither doctors nor psycho-therapists are
> taught to deal with or even bring up religious issues. [14]

Using the American Academy of Family Physicians as their source, social science commentators A. Cary and G. Visgaitis reported that 42 percent of family doctors have not been introduced to using spirituality in healing through professional training. [15] Nevertheless, 75 percent of female doctors and 63 percent of male doctors "have used prayer or meditation in treating themselves." It would be interesting to know what percentage of psychiatrists and other psychotherapists use prayer when they have healing needs. As evidenced in Larson's statements and from the Association of Unity Churches' survey, 40–50 percent of the general population and 78 percent of Unity students would like for their health care professional to pray with them about mental or physical health problems. Therefore, one might ask, "Why do psychiatrists, psychologists, and other mental health professionals not pray with their patients/clients more often?"

Four possible reasons for this come quickly to mind: (a) that a given patient/client may be one in the population who would not want the mental health professional to pray with him or her; (b) in the therapist's mind, to offer prayer might raise questions in the patient/client's mind regarding competence; (c) that the therapist and patient/client are of different religious backgrounds; and (d) that therapists do not know patient/clients would like prayer.

In response to the four scenarios noted previously, it seems appropriate that for the Unity patient (a) the mental health professional ask either on the intake questionnaire or during the first consultation whether the patient/client would want the therapist to pray with him or her; (b) the Unity patient/client will only have more confidence in the therapist's skills as the result of such an inquiry; and (c) since Unity students attempt to honor diversity, patient/client and therapist being of different religious backgrounds would tend to heighten the prayer experience together (the Unity student who had selected a therapist who was Catholic, Jewish, Muslim, or of any other religious background would consider praying with that therapist an added bonus).

It is not suggested that a physician or mental health professional proselytize or in any way apply pressure regarding religious views, but simply allow for the positive effects of coping, restoring hope, and peace that are brought about through prayer. At the very least, the psychiatrist, psychologist, or other mental health professional might ask if the Unity patient/client would like a few minutes of silence to close the consultation.

The Development of
the New Thought Movement   3

New Thought; Ancient Wisdom

G REAT SPIRITUAL TEACHINGS often contribute to uplifting the consciousness of the masses and raising levels of human awareness. The truth of one's spiritual self can be discovered through the pathway of everyday life and living. Doors may open. Opportunities often occur. The aspirant embarks on a process of discovery and ultimately recognizes a great truth—that he or she is a significant expression in the universe!

It has taken humanity perhaps thousands of years to learn that we have the ability and the power to control our destiny. Scripture tells us, "As he thinketh in his heart, so is he" (Prov. 23:7, KJV). Since thinking and the energy connected with thought represent a movement in consciousness, we begin to understand how working with the process of thinking, in alignment with universal principles, contributes greatly to the effects of our life. The thinking process is a creative force that is constantly at work in humanity.

"We live in an intelligent universe which responds to our mental states. To the extent that we learn to control these mental states, we shall automatically control our environment. This is why we study *the power of thought* as we approach the subject of spiritual mind healing,"[1] wrote Ernest Holmes, founder of the Science of Mind, a meaningful and impacting element in the unfolding New Thought movement. In Holmes's teachings, as in those of other New Thought participants, we find the distilled wisdom gleaned from many eras and many cultures and manifested in a great soul who shared his wisdom with many others.

Philosophia Perennis—a term coined by Leibniz—is a metaphysic that recognizes a divine Reality substantial to the world of things and lives and minds.[2] It is the psychology that finds something in the soul similar to, or even identical with, divine Reality. It is the ethic inherent in the knowledge of the immanent and transcendent. It is *ancient wisdom*. Ancient wisdom has inspired countless millions down through the ages. It has seeded the growth of spiritually innovative philosophies, and inspired numerous religions and their multitudinous offspring!

If one does not consider him- or herself to be a sage or a saint, then perhaps a good thing to do is to study the works of those who were. Many of the founders of the New Thought movement did just that. These great teachers (from several perspectives) then offered their wellsprings of wisdom to those individuals who gathered and walked through a central door of inspiration, dedication, and commitment into what has become an international activity involving spiritual truths. Let's take a quick look at some of these teachers, their messages, and their contributions to the New Thought movement.

Perennial Philosophers and Their Messages

New Thought has evolved as a movement that has no specific dogma to which the member religious movements must adhere. This idea stands in contrast to Christian Science, which has a more strictly outlined set of beliefs that define the organization. The first focus of the New Thought view is metaphysical healing. Secondarily, the different suborganizations place varying degrees of emphasis on the traditional Christian religious beliefs that are practiced in tandem with New Thought.

Many of the founders of the different branches of the New Thought movement were magnetic and inspiring speakers, talented authors, and prominent leaders of far-reaching vision. Although opinions regarding who actually founded New Thought vary, since the essence of the movement is rooted in the interpretation of the teachings of Phineas Parkhurst Quimby (known as "Park"), he is credited as the overall intellectual father of New Thought.

First, let's take a step back to the forerunners: Franz Anton Mesmer, Emanuel Swedenborg, Ralph Waldo Emerson, and Phineas Parkhurst Quimby.

Franz Anton Mesmer heads the chart of the evolution of the New

Thought movement. A Viennese psychiatrist, Mesmer brought forth the theory of "animal magnetism" and produced healings by the laying-on of hands, hypnosis, and suggestion, later known as Mesmerism. It is from Mesmer that we get the word *mesmerize*. He also used the armonica, a glass harmonica, as an important part of his therapy.

Emanuel Swedenborg was truly one of Europe's great minds, and it is to his thinking processes and manner of delivery that we can attribute the success of his mission as a teacher and philosopher of the Spirit. And in the late 1600s and early 1700s, Spirit needed a vehicle to help lay the groundwork for what was to follow! A respected someone who could catch the attention of the people and expand the awareness of men and women to the realities of spiritual communion and communication without creating a cultural or theological shock was needed.

Swedenborg's theology encompassed simple concepts.[3] He believed that the Bible was the Word of God; however, its true meaning differed greatly from its obvious meaning. He believed that the world of matter was a laboratory for the soul, where the material is used to "force-refine" the spiritual. In many ways, Swedenborg was quite universal in his concepts, for he believed that all religious systems have their divine duty and purpose, that this is not the sole virtue of Christianity. He believed that the mission of the church was absolutely necessary inasmuch as, left to its own devices, humanity simply could not work out its relationship to God. He saw the real power of Christ's life in the example it gave to others and vehemently rejected the concept of Christian atonement and original sin.

Ralph Waldo Emerson was an American essayist and poet and a leader of the transcendentalism movement. He was influenced by such schools of thought as English Romanticism, Neoplatonism, and Hindu philosophy. Emerson is noted for his skill in presenting his ideas eloquently and in poetic language. Several of Emerson's ancestors were ministers, including his father, William Emerson, who was minister of the First Church (Unitarian) of Boston.

Emerson graduated from Harvard University at the age of eighteen and taught school in Boston for the next three years. In 1825 he entered Harvard Divinity School and, a year later, was sanctioned to preach by the Middlesex Association of Ministers. In 1829 he became minister of the Second Church (Unitarian) of Boston. While abroad in England,

Emerson made the acquaintance of such British literary notables as Samuel Taylor Coleridge, Thomas Carlyle, and William Wordsworth. His meeting with Carlyle marked the beginning of a lifelong friendship.

Several important elements in Phineas Parkhurst Quimby's life led to the development of his ideas of mental healing. Quimby developed tuberculosis and became disillusioned with the method of treatment prescribed by his physician and gave up hope of recovery. One of his friends suggested he take up horseback riding as an outdoor physical activity to improve his condition. Physical ailments prevented him from following this suggestion, but he did the next best thing and embarked on carriage trips. This course of action produced remarkable results and his recovery prompted much thought on the matter.

Quimby began to study Mesmer and his works in 1838 after attending a lecture and began experimentation with the help of Lucius Burkmar.[4] He quickly saw the mental and placebo effect of the mind over the body and developed theories of mentally aided healing and opened an office in Portland, Maine. Quimby became so busy practicing healings that he failed to publish his writings. Among the students and patients who joined his studies and helped him commit his teachings to writings were Warren Felt Evans, Annetta Seabury Dresser, and Julius Dresser, the founders of New Thought as a named movement, and Mary Baker Eddy, the founder of the Christian Science movement. Later, in 1921, Horatio W. Dresser published the large but less than complete *The Quimby Manuscripts*. Still later, in 1988, *Phineas Parkhurst Quimby: The Complete Writings* was edited by Ervin Seale, who devoted much of his life to this task, as did his friend Errol S. Colley.

Warren Felt Evans was one of the first individuals who wrote seriously on Quimby's teachings. Although he did not establish a movement under these teachings as some other students had done, he did open a practice in Salisbury, Massachusetts. Although the most important gift that Evans left to New Thought was his written work, he also took the important step of integrating Swedenborg's and Quimby's philosophies into New Thought.

Mary Baker Eddy developed a movement out of the ideas she derived from Quimby's teachings. Through the treatment for her own poor health, Eddy became Quimby's student and began to develop her own unique ideas about metaphysical healing. In 1862 she was quickly cured after Quimby treated her.[5] In 1879, the Church of Christ, Scientist was assembled and soon ordained Eddy as the pastor.

Ernest Holmes and the Science of Mind

Ernest Holmes, born in 1887 on a small farm in Maine, was the youngest of nine sons. As a teenager, he attended Bethel preparatory school, but spent most of his time outside with nature asking the questions: "What is God? Who am I? Why am I here?"

Although religion played an important role in Holmes's family, as a youth, other than attending church and reading the Bible, he showed no strong affinity for organized religion. In fact, he mentally tangled with the local preachers and doubted the answers he received in church. He also did not excel in school. While he was an intelligent young man and showed an early interest in reading and learning, he found school itself dull and uninteresting and left his formal education before finishing high school and set out on his lifelong course of independent thinking. He went to Boston, worked in a grocery store, and pursued his studies relentlessly.

A year later, Holmes discovered the writings of Ralph Waldo Emerson. "Reading Emerson is like drinking water to me," he said later. His metaphysical studies intensified, his quest for truth leading him to literature, art, science, philosophy, and religion. In particular, he was drawn to the Christian Science teachings of Mary Baker Eddy. He soon was exploring the writings of Christian D. Larson, Ralph Waldo Trine, Horatio Dresser, and Phineas Quimby. He was particularly impressed with Larson's New Thought writings and eventually abandoned the Christian Science textbook for Larson's works.[6]

In 1914, at the age of twenty-five, Ernest moved to Venice, California. Pursuing his studies, he discovered the writings of Thomas Troward, which fed the flame ignited by Emerson and his earlier studies of metaphysics. Almost casually, he began speaking on Troward's writings to small but ever-growing groups. Without ceremony, his lifetime ministry had begun. Later, as his audiences grew, he was ordained as a minister of the Divine Science Church.

Ernest published his first book, *Creative Mind*, in 1919. He continued his studies and lectured to growing crowds in California and eastern cities. Meanwhile, he was writing *The Science of Mind*, which was to become the "textbook" of the Religious Science philosophy. Published in 1926, it was revised in 1938 and is now in its forty-fifth printing. *The Science of Mind* has been translated into French, German, and Japanese.

At the time the book was published, his many enthusiastic students urged him to set up an incorporated organization. He refused at first, but eventually agreed, and the Institute of Religious Science and the School of Philosophy was incorporated in 1927.

Also in 1927, on October 23, in Los Angeles, Ernest Holmes, at the age of forty, was married to Hazel Durkee Foster, a widow. Hazel was a wealthy, well-connected Los Angeles socialite. She became a practitioner of Holmes's work and provided invaluable support as a confidante and advisor. Her connections to well-established people in the business and entertainment community lent legitimacy to the work and contributed significantly to Holmes's success.[7] Ernest and Hazel were to be inseparable companions for thirty years. Holmes had no children, but he left all humankind an enduring legacy. It is the way of life he called Religious Science.

The Religious Science movement snowballed in the 1940s and 1950s. By the time Holmes made his transition on April 7, 1960, in Los Angeles, there were eighty-five churches spread nationwide as well as hundreds of licensed spiritual mind practitioners. Holmes never satisfactorily resolved the problems of organizing and administering a growing movement. However, he succeeded tremendously in the things he did best—preaching on Sundays, teaching his philosophy of Science of Mind, and practicing spiritual mind treatment.

Nothing in Ernest Holmes's early life suggested that he would create a new spiritual philosophy, found a church that thousands would attend, and inspire the "positive thinking" of Norman Vincent Peale, which would spread through the churches of America.[8]

Ernest Holmes's teachings are based on a belief that there is a universal law of cause and effect operating in the life of humankind that is primarily mental and spiritual. He believed that all humans have "conscious access to this law." "There is a power for good in the universe greater than you are and you can use it."[9] Dr. Holmes spoke these exact words to a group of students sharing the twentieth century with him. Because of this illustrious man and his work, countless numbers of searchers have discovered—and countless others still to come will discover—a rewarding awareness of their infinite potential.

Dr. Holmes's book, *The Science of Mind*, correlates "the laws of science, the opinions of philosophy, and the revelations of religion applied to the needs and the aspirations of humankind." This correlation, something completely new to the world, was also the beginning of the Institute of Religious Science and School of Philosophy, Inc., where he and others were to teach and inspire. This, in turn, would lead to the beginning of the Church of Religious Science, later to become the United Church of Religious Science and Religious Science International.

As Dr. Holmes always insisted, he did not legislate any of the laws that govern the universe, and he did not invent a secret new way by which humankind can partake of the unlimited good in the universe. He sought only to explain the infallibility of the laws and express the essence of the ever-existent way. In volume 1, number 1 of *Religious Science Magazine*, Ernest Holmes made this announcement:

> The purpose of this magazine will be to instruct ethically, morally, and religiously, from a scientific viewpoint of life and its meaning. A semi-religious periodical, ethical in its tendency, moral in tone, philosophical in its viewpoint, it will seek to promote that universal consciousness of life which binds all together in one great Whole. . . . It will also be the purpose of Religious Science to present to its readers a systematic and comprehensive study of the subtle powers of mind and spirit, insofar as they are now known; and to show how such powers may be consciously used for the betterment of the individual and the race.[10]

An interesting aspect of the Science of Mind is Holmes's method of prayer as a spiritual mind treatment. He wrote:

> The things we need, we are to ask for—and we are to believe that we receive them! This plumbs the very depths of the metaphysical and psychological laws of our being, and explains the possibility of an answer to our prayers. . . . *When we pray we are to believe that we have.* We are surrounded by a universal law which is creative. It moves from the thought to the thing. Unless there is first an image, it cannot move, for there would be nothing for it to move toward. Prayer, which is a mental act, must accept its own answer as an

image in the mind, before the divine energies can play upon it and make it productive. . . . But let us remember that true prayer is always universal. There can be no good to us alone, only as that good is for all.[11]

When Holmes was once asked upon what authority his teaching was based, he referred the questioner to Jesus, who, when asked the same question, said that the authority of his words was in his works. "There is no authority for Science of Mind," said Holmes, "other than what it accomplished." The serious student of Science of Mind will discover "that it teaches a principle that can be demonstrated, that its authority is not in its words, but in what it can accomplish."[12]

In beautiful writings that are powerful and precise, *The Science of Mind* offers a blueprint for the remaking of the mind, redirecting the thought processes, and granting the individual tremendous ability to construct our world through the extraordinary working power of our minds. Holmes's philosophy incorporates two routes to our mind's yearning to know what is so: Those who know themselves comprehend the universe, and those who know the universe comprehend themselves!

As we remain open to growth on all levels of our being, we avoid diminishment. We become aware that we may represent the music of life, but the Creator is the Master Musician.

The International New Thought Alliance

The International New Thought Alliance (INTA) is an umbrella organization facilitating the functioning of numerous branches, organizations, and individuals of the more than century-old New Thought movement. New Thought is a positive approach to living that emphasizes the practice of the presence of God for practical purposes. Among the branches of New Thought are Unity, Religious Science (Science of Mind), and Divine Science.

The first INTA Congress was held in 1914 in London, England. Since then, through 2005, eighty-nine additional congresses have been held in locations around the world. The list of chairpersons for these congresses reads like a New Thought "Who's Who."

The purposes of the INTA are outlined in its bylaws:

1. Promoting spiritual inspiration and guidance for ministers, other leaders, and laity;
2. Offering international and local programs designed to aid understanding of New Thought and to promote interest in it;
3. Providing support groups for emotional and spiritual renewal;
4. Encouraging educational excellence throughout the New Thought movement in INTA meetings, educational institutions, programs, and local teaching; and
5. Developing connections between New Thought and a wide variety of scholarly and other associations that should know about New Thought increasingly and understand and appreciate it. INTA's overall purposes are to preserve New Thought's rich heritage through archival and other work, to promote the effectiveness of New Thought practices, to encourage the constant rethinking of its theoretical foundations, to help all New Thoughters to grow in their awareness and love of God, to do all appropriate to secure a prominent place for New Thought in the world's approaches to reality, and to be of appropriate service to the world in achieving peace, prosperity, and wellness in all dimensions of existence.

In short, INTA is deeply concerned with what in industry would be called "research and development," as well as "distribution" around the world!

The INTA Declaration of Principles is as follows:
1. We affirm God as Mind, Infinite Being, Spirit, Ultimate Reality.
2. We affirm God, the Good, is supreme, universal, and everlasting.
3. We affirm the unity of God and humanity, in that the divine nature dwells within and expresses through each of us, by means of our acceptance of it, as health, supply, wisdom, love, life, truth, power, beauty, and peace.
4. We affirm the power of prayer and the capacity of each person to have mystical experience with God, and to enjoy the grace of God.
5. We affirm the freedom of all persons as to beliefs, and we honor the diversity of humanity by being open and affirming of all persons, affirming the dignity of human beings as founded on the presence of God.
6. We affirm that we are all spiritual beings, dwelling in a spiritual

universe, that is governed by spiritual law, and that in alignment
with spiritual law, we can heal, prosper, and harmonize.

7. We affirm that our mental states are carried forward into manifestation and become our experience in daily living.

8. We affirm the manifestation of the kingdom of heaven here and
now.

9. We affirm the expression of the highest spiritual principle in loving one another unconditionally, promoting the highest good for
all, teaching and healing one another, ministering to one another,
and living together in peace, in accordance with the teachings of
Jesus and other enlightened teachers.

10. We affirm our evolving awareness of the nature of reality and our
willingness to refine our beliefs accordingly.

Later New Thought Leaders

Dr. Masaharu Taniguchi was known as the "Miracle Man of Japan" and
founded the Truth of Life Movement of *Seicho-No-Ie* in 1930. Dr.
Taniguchi held a deep inborn love and compassion for humanity and was
deeply concerned over the contradiction in life, and his heart was troubled with the suffering of humankind. He studied many philosophies,
both old and new, of the East and of the West, seeking answers to the
problems common to all people: "What is man?" or "What is the meaning of life?" After extensive study, contemplation, and while in deep meditation, the new light—the Truth—was directly revealed to him.

This realization came as if it were a commanding voice: "All evil things
are nothingness. They could never be the product of Divine Will but of
man's deluded mind." After this revelation, Dr. Taniguchi developed a
marvelous healing power and many were healed of their disease merely
by listening to his lecture or by receiving his visit.

An interesting story is told that at the time of Dr. Taniguchi's revelation, he held a position as an English translator with a certain business
firm. He began to save portions of his income in anticipation of the day
when he could begin publishing a nondenominational truth magazine.
However, soon after he had saved a certain amount, he fell victim to a
theft. He searched within himself for the answer to this problem, and
heard intuitively a heavenly voice saying, "The world is a reflection of the

mind. The source of all necessary supply is already within you. Rise now! Begin your mission now!"[13]

Immediately after this inspiration he published the first issue of his magazine, *Seicho-No-Ie*. Surprisingly, this magazine brought another sequence of healings to the readers. People began to realize that this spiritual movement was, indeed, divinely founded and guided by spirit in order to help humanity. Under his direct leadership, Seicho-No-Ie, a nondenominational religion, grew into an extensive religious movement with over five million followers.

During these days of tremendous social change, many are seeking new and effective ways of coping with everyday living and ways to bring needed socioeconomic change to the world. The message of practical Christianity can bring a message of hope for people all over the world.

Another New Thought leader is Reverend Dr. Johnnie Colemon, founder of Christ Universal Temple in Chicago, Illinois. Often referred to as the "first lady of America's religious community," she brings a message of hope, peace, love, joy, and happiness. Christ Universal Temple is a teaching ministry that inspires and empowers people to live from the divine potential within them, thereby meeting the needs of the total person. Christ Universal Temple is a thriving, spirited, and progressive New Thought church with more than 20,000 members. The Temple's philosophy is not to attempt to teach a person *what* to think, rather, to teach one *how* to think so the individual may go forth and experience a revelation of Truth that is right for him or her.

Dr. Colemon's book, *Open Your Mind and Be Healed*, tells her remarkable personal story along with describing universal principles of healing. After learning she had an incurable disease (1953), Dr. Colemon enrolled in the Unity School of Christianity in Lee's Summit, Missouri, where she received her teaching certificate and became an ordained minister. Always a trailblazer, Dr. Colemon pioneered many "firsts." Out of a sense of knowing that a need for a vital, new affiliation of independent New Thought churches existed, Dr. Colemon's dynamic leadership led to the organization of the Universal Foundation for Better Living, Inc. Her message is simple: "God's desire for everyone is absolute good." And many have been molded, shaped, and inspired by Dr. Colemon's insightful and loving instruction.

In addition to serving as district president for the International New

Thought Alliance and president of the Association of Unity Churches, International, Dr. Colemon has been a pioneer in the media ministry, hosting a weekly telecast that aired in nine markets during the 1970s. She continues to be the subject of feature articles in major print publications and is a popular guest on radio and television.

Dr. Barbara Lewis King is another outstanding leader in the New Thought movement. Founder and minister of the Hillside International Chapel and Truth Center, Inc. in Atlanta, Georgia, Barbara began this nondenominational, ecumenical ministry in 1971 in her living room with twelve members. Now, the Hillside International Chapel and Truth Center incorporates nearly twelve acres with a growing congregation numbering more than 10,000!

Dr. King, a native of Houston, Texas, was raised as a member of the legendary Antioch Baptist Church. Drawing from her extensive spiritual history and rich background, Dr. King's ministry has extended throughout the world. She has traveled extensively in the United States and many other countries, including Finland, Russia, England, Israel, Egypt, Kenya, Senegal, South Africa, the Caribbean, Brazil, and British Guyana. Her universal appeal, coupled with Hillside's espousal of international ministry, makes it appropriate that Hillside Chapel was the first African American New Thought affiliate to establish a sister church in South Africa. The South Africa branch was ordained in May 1994. Beyond a busy speaking schedule, Dr. King is author of several books and contributes to the activities of the International New Thought Alliance.

A review of modern-day New Thought leaders wouldn't be complete without touching on the work of Dr. Michael Beckwith, founder and spiritual director of Agape International Spiritual Center in Culver City, California. Dr. Beckwith held a visioning meeting in his home with approximately twenty people in attendance. The purpose of this meeting was to become, in consciousness, the kind of church they would want to attend. In 1986 Dr. Beckwith's inner vision revealed a world united on an ethical basis of humankind's highest spiritual and social development. Today Agape is a spiritual community of God with outreach programs that care for the Agape community, the community of the city, the country, and the world.

The Agape Church is one of the largest multicultural churches of its kind in the United States. It has been said that walking into a service at

Agape is like walking into the United Nations. Michael's commitment as a world citizen is evidenced by his position as founding member and president of the Association for Global New Thought, convening organization of the annual Synthesis Dialogues with His Holiness, the Dalai Lama, and as an elected assembly member of the Parliament of the World's Religions.

Further evidence of Michael Beckwith's "world-influencing consciousness" is a guided visioning process he facilitated after the Leadership Council of the Association for Global New Thought had met with His Holiness, the Dalai Lama, in Rome in June 2004. It feels deeply meaningful to share part of Michael's process with you in the next section.

Synthesis Dialogues: What Visions and Actions Will Catalyze the Emergence of a Culture of Consciousness?[14]

Michael Beckwith guided us through a visioning process during which we considered the following questions within the greater context of our conversations up to this point:

Question: What are the emerging principles of evolving global awareness?

Question: What are models, metaphors, and methodologies for awakening in our fields?

Question: What do we hold as the essential elements of the needed synthesis?

Question: Is there a social and mystical technology of synthesis?

Question: What is my commitment to this work?

Question: What shall we do—in action?

In response, the group synthesized its visions of some universal principles, guiding insights, practices, commitments, and technologies that will catalyze the emergence of a culture of consciousness. Not ironically, when looking for a framework into which I might embed our collective wisdom, I found that the Noble Eight-fold Path of the Buddhist tradition worked quite well.

Since many of our insights easily cross categories, please feel free to edit and rearrange my structural choices as a way of engaging in our continuing dialogue!

It would be very interesting if those among us with knowledge of parallel systems in Christianity, Islam, New Thought, Suffism, Native American, Bahai'i, scientific, economic, and other traditions would care to submit them into dialogue with reference to the notes from our visioning process. Synthesis benefits from articulating "precise universalities."

The Noble Eightfold Path

The Noble Eightfold Path describes the way to the end of suffering, as it was laid out by Siddhartha Gautama. It is a practical guideline to ethical and mental development with the goal of freeing the individual from attachments and delusions; and it finally leads to understanding the truth about all things. Together with the Four Noble Truths, it constitutes the gist of Buddhism. Great emphasis is put on the practical aspect, because it is only through practice that one can attain a higher level of existence and finally reach Nirvana. The eight aspects of the path are not to be understood as a sequence of single steps, instead, they are highly interdependent principles that have to be seen in relationship with each other.

WISDOM

1. *Right View.* Right view is the beginning and the end of the path. It simply means to see and to understand things as they really are and to realize the Four Noble Truths. As such, right view is the cognitive aspect of wisdom. It means to see things through, to grasp the impermanent and imperfect nature of worldly objects and ideas, and to understand the law of karma and karmic conditioning. Right view is not necessarily an intellectual capacity, just as wisdom is not just a matter of intelligence. Instead, right view is attained, sustained, and enhanced through all capacities of mind.

Comments from the Synthesis Dialogues:

- ▸ To reconnect individuals to our innate nature.
- ▸ There is nothing quite so painful as a broken heart. But a broken heart is an open heart. If you can learn to live with an open heart, gentle transformations begin to occur.
- ▸ To be conscious at every moment of our inner identity of loving-kindness, and by this become known to friend and foe alike.
- ▸ Enable methods to synthesize thought and action and bring the balance to the center of our work.
- ▸ Change the story wherein Science has been elevated to the Priesthood. Revisit the truth of our observations of the natural world in order to create a more accurate and hopeful scientific story that integrates phenomenology with spirit in sustainable abundance.

2. *Right Intention.* While right view refers to the cognitive aspect of wisdom, right intention refers to the volitional aspect, i.e., the kind of mental energy that controls our actions. Right intention can be described as *commitment* to ethical and mental self-improvement. Foremost is the intention of harmlessness, meaning not to think or act cruelly, violently, or aggressively, and to develop compassion.

Comments from the Synthesis Dialogues:

- ▸ To spread goodwill.
- ▸ To struggle nonviolently for nonviolence
- ▸ Acknowledge that things are "not right."
- ▸ The principles of evolving awareness:
  - ▸ To embrace Precise Simplicity (specify means and methods).
  - ▸ To be non-judgmental.
  - ▸ To be truly universal.
  - ▸ To embody our Collective Interdependence.

ETHICAL CONDUCT

3. *Right Speech.* Right speech is the first principle of ethical conduct in the Eightfold Path. Ethical conduct is viewed as a guideline to moral discipline, which supports the other principles of the path. This aspect is not self-sufficient, however, essential, because mental purification can only be achieved through the cultivation of ethical

conduct. The importance of speech in the context of Buddhist ethics is obvious: words can break or save lives, make enemies or friends, start war or create peace.

Comments from the Synthesis Dialogues:

▶ Those in power must be told the truth in a way that will be heard.

▶ In order to acknowledge what is wrong, we must find our holy "No" to injustice. Emphasizing only affirmation precludes the necessity in these hard times for sacred negation in engaging complex and intractable injustice. Synthesis must be preceded by proper differentiation of Yes/No and a Third Side.

▶ To voice clearly: Yes/No/Wait a minute!

4. *Right Action.* The second ethical principle, right action, involves the body as natural means of expression, as it refers to deeds that involve manifestation through actions. Unwholesome actions lead to unsound states of mind, while wholesome actions lead to sound states of mind. Positively formulated, right action means to act kindly and compassionately, to be honest, to respect others, and to keep relationships harmless to others.

Comments from the Synthesis Dialogues:

▶ Make a commitment to change.

▶ To anchor the notion of our shared destiny, with emphasis on human dignity, and empathy for the plight of the impoverished in order to ease it.

▶ Action motivated by need to prove our own existence is not enough.

▶ Principles of evolving awareness are to be found in Dr. Martin Luther King's definition of the "beloved community."

▶ Methodologies of awakening begin with education, ethics and spirituality of the inner person.

▶ Help our children understand the true meaning of "Power beyond hierarchy, class distinctions, and domination of the overpowered above the dispossessed and disenfranchised."

5. *Right Livelihood.* Right livelihood means that one should earn one's living in a righteous way and that wealth should be gained legally and peacefully. Furthermore, any other occupation that

would violate the principles of right speech and right action should be avoided.

Comments from the Synthesis Dialogues:

► To give and receive with authenticity.

► Knowing when to stop "business as usual," because we are not applying our efforts to the right business for cultural change.

► Ask the Gandhian question: "Will it benefit the weakest and poorest among us?"

► Models and methodologies of evolving awareness:

  ► To live the experience that matter and non-matter are one.

  ► To recognize the fundamentals of spiritual capital and bring them into our economic thinking and government policies.

  ► Infuse meme of interdependence into the value system of our economics so that spiritual riches are prized over the material.

MENTAL DEVELOPMENT

6. *Right Effort*. Right effort can be seen as a prerequisite for the other principles of the path. Without effort, which is in itself an act of will, nothing can be achieved, whereas misguided effort distracts the mind from its task, and confusion will be the consequence. Mental energy is the force behind right effort. The same type of energy that fuels desire, envy, aggression, and violence can, on the other side, fuel self-discipline, honesty, benevolence, and kindness.

Comments from the Synthesis Dialogues:

► To promote education, interest, and respect.

► To respect, protect, and awaken all life.

► To base every interaction on Right Relationship; to develop technologies to evolve social and emotional learning.

► Any social and mystical technology of synthesis must "back away" from the external to internal process; turn to cultivation of neglected internal technologies such as character, virtue, truth-telling, courage, compassion.

7. *Right Mindfulness*. Right mindfulness is the controlled and perfected faculty of cognition. It is the mental ability to see things as

they are, with clear consciousness. Usually, the cognitive process begins with an impression induced by perception, or by a thought, but then it does not stay with the mere impression. Instead, we almost always conceptualize sense impressions and thoughts immediately. We interpret them and set them in motion to other thoughts and experiences, which naturally go beyond the factuality of the original impression. The mind then posits concepts, joins concepts into constructs, and weaves those constructs into complex interpretative schemes. All this happens only half consciously, and as a result, we often see things obscured. Right mindfulness is anchored in clear perception and it penetrates impressions without getting carried away. Right mindfulness enables us to be aware of the process of conceptualization in a way that we actively observe and control the way our thoughts go.

Comments from the Synthesis Dialogues:

▶ Think as "we" instead of "me." How do we live as one humanity and how far are we, indeed, from actualizing this vision?

▶ To be open to the Now, leaving behind the certainty of what we already know.

▶ Technologies: Synthesis arises when belief systems are annihilated in that they are lenses distorting reality. Meditation can facilitate the power of our commitment to this work.

8. *Right Concentration.* The eighth principle of the path, right concentration, refers to the development of a mental force that occurs in natural consciousness, although at a relatively low level of intensity, namely concentration. Concentration in this context is described as one pointedness of mind, meaning a state where all mental facilities are unified and directed toward a unified goal.

Comments from the Synthesis Dialogues:

▶ Hold awareness that ignorance generates ignorance and wisdom procreates wisdom.

▶ Thousands of people come together in prayer and meditation as a "technology" to effect change. Humanity seen as a *psychosphere* will allow the noblest in us to emerge, regardless of geography.

A sought-after meditation teacher, Dr. Beckwith is the author of *40 Day Mind Fast—Soul Feast and A Manifesto of Peace*. Perhaps an insight into Dr. Beckwith's credo can best be described in his own words: "Speaking for myself, what I know to do is to keep meditating, keep praying, keep opening my heart wider and wider, keep listening more deeply. I am going to love more profoundly and express more passionately. This is my contribution as I walk the path of an emissary of peace, a cosmic citizen. I am committed to being, saying, and doing what is necessary to create the kind of world I want to live in."[15]

At the Forefront of a Spiritual Revolution

Remember *Megatrends 2000* by John Naisbitt and Patricia Aburdene?[16] They were the most noted of authors who, in the 1990s (in that long-gone last millennium), suggested that Unity was the religious wave of the future. I feel sure they would now include all New Thought movements in this assessment. They were right, I believe, but I think it may not be in quite the way that even these far-sighted futurists envisioned. They saw us having a unique message—we stood out when they wrote *Megatrends* because of our message.

Much of what we have taught has been revised, adapted, improved upon, or adopted wholly by many organizations and institutions. Some of them are religious; some of them are social, psychological, or educational (religious and secular). Some are even scientific institutions and medical researchers. Some are corporate. The corporate world might have been expected to be the least of those in the spiritual revolution that the world is in the midst of but, in fact, many corporations are now among the leaders.

According to *Business Week*, for instance, Xerox Corporation employees from senior managers to entry-level clerks participate in "vision quests" as part of their project to revolutionize product development. Their success inspired Ford Motor Company, Nike, and Harley David-son to investigate their results.

Taco Bell, Pizza Hut, and Wal-Mart subsidiaries provide employees with "God-Squad" people to help in time of need. Talking about God in the workplace is no longer a prerogative of the fundamentalist only.

Deloitte & Touche have prayer groups and New York law firms have studies in the Talmud. All of this and much more is a part of a much broader trend—the spiritual revolution that is definitely not being led by the traditional church.

In Unity, the Association of Unity Churches, International has been working with the idea of a Noble Purpose Project. As an example, we now have an annual award for a domestic or international for-profit business practicing spiritual principles in the workplace. Many Unity and other New Thought churches are active in a wide variety of community outreach programs that appropriately come under the heading of "faith-based initiatives."

New Thought has historically been at the forefront of spiritual revolution, but we dare not let it just pass us by. We need to remain at the forefront of influence into the consciousness of humankind.

New Thought philosophy and teachings are being folded into other denominations as well. The common denominator among the mega-churches of the Methodists, Lutherans, Congregationalists, Episcopalians, Dutch Reform, and Presbyterians is that their messages all sound like each other and they all have a "New Thought ring" to them. Most important to note is that they do not sound like the denomination they represent. It is no accident that almost no one knew that Norman Vincent Peale was Dutch Reform or that Robert Schuller is Dutch Reform.

Naisbitt, I believe, foresaw New Thought as a major force in societal-religious change, but largely while acting like a denomination. Most of us have colleagues with whom we've discussed the question: Is New Thought denominational or not?

Perhaps those of us who are part of the New Thought movement would be served well by not trying to "lock us in" to a position, but to look beyond to what more we are. The *Trends Journal* predicts people will find fresh answers in a new faith movement that mixes Eastern thought, Western religion, mysticism, and native teachings.

For a movement such as New Thought that has admittedly been influenced by large segments of some of the world's eight great religions (Islam, Confucianism, Hinduism, Judaism, Christianity, Buddhism, Taoism, and worldwide indigenous religions—not just American Native spirituality), we are well positioned to go beyond being "just another denomination" to being denominations (if we insist), but so much more if we can envision it.

Trends Journal also has suggested that traditional faiths will not like the new movement and will call its leaders heretics. However, the new spirituality avoids the sociopolitical and moral issues of denominationalism, but will instead "focus on the spiritual development that brings people closer to the peace and salvation they seek."

At least one path that will lead people to this peace is the move from what has been called the "Hero's Journey" to the "Tribal Journey." In short, for ministers and spiritual leaders this means capacity-building of the people who show up at our churches.

Many people who first come to New Thought do so because they are desperate and in some cases are no longer welcome in their former houses of worship. Not just a few attend New Thought groups until they get the "healing, job, or relationship" they came to get and then leave. I believe that encouraging membership is okay, but it's much more important to inspire them with a commitment to share in the ministry. Just as people in the anonymous self-help groups are taught to come get their help and to stay to help those who follow them, I think we need to inspire the New Thought attendee to do likewise. This is shifting from the "Hero's—you are the minister or spiritual leader—journey" to the "Tribal (congregant or attendee) journey." Many members and attendees, while not interested in sociopolitical denominationalism, are interested and willing to serve with you in doing ministry. They only need to be invited (trained in the part of ministry that appeals to them), and then to be put to work ministering.

In this new millennium, we in New Thought may be "denominations" and we are so much more.

Matthew Fox University of Creation Spirituality and Wisdom University

Matthew Fox is truly a mystic, both from ancient wisdom and from the modern era. He created the University of Creation Spirituality, and was its exceptionally creative president for eight years before officially handing over the presidency to Jim Garrison at the spring equinox, 2005 C.E.

At the same time, the University changed its name to Wisdom University. Matthew, a former Catholic priest and now an Episcopal priest, will remain fully engaged as the University's president emeritus and its creative director.

Because Matthew Fox and Wisdom University and, to all appearances, Jim Garrison, all epitomize the ancient wisdom traditions and have a fascinating way of bringing that wisdom to shine in the dimly lighted corners of our present world, they clearly belong alongside, and more, they clearly belong *to* the genre of New Thought and ancient wisdom believers, followers and leaders.

The following information is largely in the words of Matthew Fox and Jim Garrison at the dawning of a new era in the history of an important institution of wisdom, the University of Creation Spirituality, as it fully becomes Wisdom University.

With permission and grateful appreciation, we share the following from Matthew Fox.[17]

A Thought on University of Creation Spirituality (UCS) from Matthew Fox

I have heard a few concerns about UCS changing its name. Yet over the years I have heard more concerns about how difficult it is to "explain" the name, "University of Creation Spirituality," in a few words—how one has to tell people we are NOT about "creationism," how the CS (creation spirituality) tradition is not this but is so-and-so, etc. etc.

I believe the change to "Wisdom University" is the right way to go. One does not have to spend a lot of time on explaining what is meant; yet it arouses interest. There is a seamless transition from UCS to Wisdom University because, as every student of creation spirituality knows, CS is the wisdom tradition of the West. It is also the tradition of the historical Jesus (scholars from the Jesus Seminar like Marcus Borg, Dominic Crossan, Bruce Chilton, and more agree to that)—and, to be honest, I have been saying this for many years long before the Jesus seminar people finally spoke out. As I pointed out in "The Coming of the Cosmic Christ," Cosmic Wisdom is a synonym for Cosmic Christ. . . .

Consider, too, how the very first page of *Original Blessing*, written as a "primer in creation spirituality," is all about wisdom. The title of the Introduction is: "Two Questions Apropos of Wisdom and Human/Earth Survival," and I lay out the entire argument for CS on the basis of the search for wisdom and how the CS tradition represents such a tradition. I also cite E. F. Schumacher in that first page for his observation that wisdom is found in two places: nature and religious traditions.

I think Jim Garrison, in the following document, makes strong arguments about how what we have been about for years as UCS and where we can go now as Wisdom University places us in the midst of the political-historical-religious struggle of our times . . .

So, I am fully on board professionally and personally with this switch and to me it represents the bigger switch that UCS is undergoing: Our moving from our eight years (really, 28 years) of testing and start-up to our coming into a more mature role as a true cultural influence on a larger scale. I believe Jim's vision and contacts, combined with the hard work invested by so many in creating this vessel called UCS over the past eight years (and the twenty years that preceded that in its other incarnations), are bringing UCS and now Wisdom University to its true potential as a vessel for gathering wisdom and a challenger to corrupted power whether of religion, academia or other places.

I believe the name, "Wisdom University," will more easily facilitate our role of interfering, that is our prophetic role, at the same time that it gets to the essence of what we are about—recovering the wisdom and mystical traditions of the West and allying them (including science) to wisdom traditions of the East and of indigenous peoples. . . .

Wisdom University
By Jim Garrison, President

As the twenty-first century unfolds, there is a critical need for a new way of thinking and acting that applies ancient wisdom to contemporary challenges. In this spirit, the University of Creation Spirituality, founded in 1996 by Matthew Fox and now led by its new President, Jim Garrison, is changing its name to Wisdom

University. In an integrating world, wisdom, which the University understands as the integration of intelligence and compassion, needs to be globalized and creatively applied in the market-place of ideas and events shaping the world in order for humanity to build a truly humane global civilization. A sustainable civilization will be a wisdom civilization.

Matthew Fox developed the theology of Creation Spirituality as a way to integrate the wisdom of western spirituality and global indigenous cultures with the emerging scientific understanding of the universe and the creativity of art. Creation Spirituality has its roots in the earliest formulations of the Judeo-Christian wisdom tradition, celebrated by the mystics of this tradition ever since, especially in medieval Europe. Creation Spirituality thus provides a holistic perspective from which to address the critical issues of our times, including the revitalization of religion and culture, the honoring of the feminine, the celebration of hope, the promotion of social and ecological justice and the promotion of interfaith understanding. In pursuing these goals, Creation Spirituality has sought to revitalize education, ritual, work and spirituality in the spirit of what Fox calls "deep ecumenism."

Wisdom University seeks to build on the curriculum related to Creation Spirituality developed by Fox over the past twenty-eight years, as well as the graduate program in "Indigenous Mind" developed by Dr. Apela Colorado, a curator of indigenous traditions worldwide. Wisdom University also intends to deepen its exploration and pedagogy in the wisdom domain by further developing programs in all the major world traditions as well as what philosopher Peter Kingsley calls "primordial wisdom."

In this spirit, the University intends to:

Broaden its curriculum, both on-site and through distance learning, to encompass a comprehensive study of wisdom and to inquire how engaged wisdom can catalyze new forms of spirituality and innovative solutions to contemporary challenges;

Establish a global network of institutions dedicated to the mutual exchange of ancient and contemporary wisdom;

Identify wisdom teachers around the world who would be invited to offer courses and instruction;

    Convene conferences and research projects on how the various
    aspects of the world's wisdom traditions can inform the for-
    mation of a wisdom civilization.

THE IMPORTANCE OF WISDOM IN AN
INTEGRATING WORLD

The reason wisdom has become so critical for contemporary society is that we are in an era of unprecedented integration framed
within the reality of escalating uncertainty. Humanity has reached
a moment in time when sharing its physical and spiritual resources
has become an urgent historical imperative. Wisdom University,
almost alone among world institutions, views wisdom as a natural
resource. Even as water, earth and air are resources of the earth,
wisdom is a resource of the spirit and must be recognized and hon-
ored as such. Nurturing and sharing the wisdom traditions common to all humanity can assist us in raising ourselves out of the
current morass of mistrust and turmoil to act more humanely with
one another and more sustainable with our earth as we fashion the
first global civilization.

    This enterprise could make a critical contribution to human dia-
logue and understanding, for what challenges global integration as
the twenty-first century unfolds is not so much a clash of civiliza-
tions as a clash of fundamentalisms. In all of the world's major religions, which so dramatically influence political ideologies and
social affairs, there is a tension between fundamentalists who
emphasize a sectarian aspect and others who emphasize a wisdom
aspect. It is between these two poles that world views are formulated, political action motivated, and the great conversation concerning what it means to be human in an unfathomable universe
takes shape.

    Fundamentalism divides the world into "us" and "them." It is con-
cerned with how to belong to an "in" group separated from other
groups by certain commonly held beliefs and rituals. The Abra-
hamic religions, in particular—Judaism, Christianity, and Islam—
are to significant extent currently gripped by the divisiveness and
sectarianism inherent in their fundamentalist traditions. . . .

These three fundamentalist traditions are absolutely sure of their theological correctness, are inserting themselves aggressively in the political process and are convinced of their ultimate earthly as well as cosmic triumph. Their interaction is contributing to the spiral of destruction and hate that is threatening the entire Middle East with conflagration. Religious and ethnic fundamentalism is also present in parts of Africa, in Hinduism and in Japan. Its divisive dogmatism upsets the moral and socio-political equilibrium of the world.

Against this fundamentalist trend stands wisdom. In the wisdom traditions, the issue is not how to be "saved" or how to defeat the "infidel." The focus of wisdom is how to live in harmony with nature and all other sentient beings. Wisdom in all the great religious traditions concerns the process by which one comes to identify with the whole human community and to understand values common to all humanity. It is that aspect of human reflection that emphasizes the process of personal and communal transformation within a divine presence that encompasses all life and is available to all who seek its transformative power. In Judaism, for instance, this understanding is expressed as "Sophia." In Christianity, it is expressed as the "Cosmic Christ." In Islam, Sufism has refined this awareness. Wisdom traditions have thus always had a dialectical relationship with the strictures of sect and ritual. For wisdom traditions, there is no "in" group. There is only the transformative experience of mystery symbolized by the alchemical process of transforming base metal into gold.

As the twenty-first century unfolds, therefore, we bear witness to a great struggle between nation states and armed groups intent on conflict and destruction. This struggle has many social, political, and environmental causes and repercussions. Under-girding and shaping this complexity lies a religious and cultural tension between those who emphasize the exclusivity of sect and those who embrace the inclusivity of wisdom. It is between literalist and non-literalist, between the fundamentalists and the universalists, between those who seek distinctions in order to divide and those who seek commonalities in order to unite.

Illuminating wisdom in this time of intolerance, terrorism and conflict will not be an easy process. The endeavor will be fraught with difficulties and dangers. There are many forces, institutions and leaders who are motivated by the acquisition of power and have much invested in sectarian divisions and the politics of fear. We are thus in a time of over-weaning pride and the willingness to use force, a time of competition, exclusion and degradation of community and the environment alike.

What is needed more than anything else is a sense of interdependence, of proportion, or humility in the face of life's complexities and human diversity. It is not an over-statement to say that in this time of both crisis and opportunity, wisdom can illuminate the way. Wisdom may, in the end, be humanity's only source of peace and hope. It is the most precious natural resource we have, for depending on how we embrace and apply it, all other resources, indeed human relations itself, are affected for good or for ill.

Using wisdom to fashion the future paradoxically harks back to the earliest days of human reflection upon how to live with intelligence and compassion in an impermanent and unpredictable world. In antiquity, the Greek schools of Parmenides and Empedocles as well as the academies of Pythagoras, Plato, and Aristotle were wisdom schools. Indeed, the very meaning of philosopher, a Greek word, is "lover of wisdom." Wisdom schools also flourished in ancient Rome, Egypt, Mesopotamia, India and China.

These schools were the precursors to what came into full bloom in twelfth-century Islam and in Europe: schools which began to call themselves "university," from the Latin *universitas,* meaning cosmic order or harmony. When the great Scholastic theologian, Thomas Aquinas, gave his inaugural lecture at the very first university, the University of Paris, he chose wisdom as his topic. In that first university, as in antiquity, wisdom was considered the queen of the sciences.

For the ancient wisdom schools as well as for the earliest universities, the quest for cosmic order, expressed as justice, lay at the center of their learning. Thus, the "is-ness" and the "ought-ness" of life were understood as integral to one another. Virtue was inherent in and inseparable from truth, beauty and goodness. Compassion without intelligence was seen as little more than sentiment, often divisive. Intelligence without compassion was seen as cold and indifferent, often cruel. The integration of compassion and intelligence was seen as the wellspring of wisdom.

This was true then. It is true today. It was to deepen the exploration of this "perennial wisdom" that UCS was founded by one of our great contemporary mystics, Matthew Fox. The institution now seeks to further illumine this domain by becoming Wisdom University, with a mission to develop a curriculum that encompasses the full spectrum of wisdom studies, both past and present, and wisdom engaged, both spiritually and politically. Such dimensionality lies at the heart of the wisdom civilization for which humanity has yearned since the beginning of its earthly journey.

We welcome the past of the University of Creation Spirituality, the present, and the future as Wisdom University, along with Matthew Fox and Jim Garrison as major strengths and leaders in carrying and casting the light so that others, all of us, may see more clearly ways of applying ancient wisdom to present-day challenges.

Unity and New Thought

New Thought and Unity share many of the same guiding principles: the centrality of mind, the focus upon the immanence of God and the divine within, the clear distinction between Jesus of history and the Christ, and the practice of metaphysical healing. As a result, many teachers whose works are based on New Thought themes and principles and who identify themselves as part of the New Thought movement hold Unity in high regard and acknowledge Unity for the contribution it has made to spirituality in the twentieth century.[18] Two of the most influential supporters were Emmet Fox, a prolific author, and Dr. Norman Vincent Peale of New York City's Marble Collegiate Church. In a lecture at Unity Village in 1972, Dr. Peale stated, "I have been spiritually fed by this place for many years. I am personally glad to acknowledge the debt of gratitude that I owe to Unity for many spiritual insights and growth, and for the help that it has given me in my ministry over the years."[19] Also, in a lecture at Unity Village at the Ministers' Conference in 1964, Dr. Peale said, "I consider Charles Fillmore to be my spiritual father."

So where do we go from here? As a movement, Unity faces a variety of perspectives as it proceeds further into the twenty-first century. Certainly there is a continued commitment to provide the prayer ministry and spiritual healing work through Silent Unity that brings widespread benefits to a wide range of constituents, both Unity and non-Unity members. The ministerial training program offered through the Unity Institute equips its graduates for leadership in Unity ministries. Another pathway to ministerial leadership is the Field Licensing Program conducted by the Association of Unity Churches, International. Both of these programs continue to work toward cutting a major swath across the consciousness of humankind. In a cooperative way, both of the programs receive input from both Unity and the Association of Unity Churches, International.

The New Thought message has been, in a sea of troubled waters, a rock. Now it is a seed upon the wind, taking root in numerous traditional religions; they often are difficult to distinguish from New Thought ministries.

Internationalization of Unity and New Thought

The Association of Unity Churches, International continues to evolve in a committed way to serving all international Unity ministries and through alliances with all New Thought ministries in whatever ways we can serve, for example, "The path to peacemaking," management consultancy, and so on.

Vision and mission are the stars by which we, the Association membership, steer our organization. We have been international from our inception in 1966, and through the years have taken on increasing roles and responsibilities for insuring that all internationals (including Americans who are also international) involved with us have their voices heard and their votes counted. We have a mission to help capacity-build every nation so that its efforts may increase and bear fruit abundantly.

The primary phenomenon we want to avoid is internationalization, which is imperialization. In other words, we continue moving into the garden of growth with a willingness to sow and to harvest; to be sown and to be harvested.

The caveat is that, although the desire to believe otherwise is sometimes strong, no one "carries the light" from the West to the East nor from the East to the West; not from North to South nor the other way 'round! Each person, each group, religious, scientific, or otherwise, and each nation has her/his/their own lights. The solution and what is required to help in the igniting of the light is developing the existing rich resources within people and in all cultures interested in joining with those of us who have already self-identified in countries the world over. In this, we are all together in our efforts to help where and when we can, and to refrain from helping where help is clearly not needed. In short, our challenge is to go "glocal" (not a misspelling!).

To see where we have been and to see where we are, as well as where we're heading, let's take a look at some numbers. In January 1985, there were 440 Unity ministries worldwide, mostly in the United States, Canada, and Nigeria. On April 30, 2001, there were three Associations of Unity Churches; the Canadian and Nigerian associations were national and the United States was international. Organizationally, these three associations were not, and are not, monoliths. We still have one international association and, since May 1, 2001, the movements in several countries have created their own national associations. Added to the Canadian and Nigerian associations are ten more Associations of Unity Leadership, in Argentina, Australia, Colombia, Cuba, Dominican Republic, Ghana, Guyana, Jamaica, Mexico, and the United Kingdom— a total of thirteen in mid-2005.

On April 30, 2001, there were four schools for Unity leadership. There were national schools in Nigeria and Puerto Rico and two international programs for leadership in the United States. Since May 1, 2001, we have added twelve more such schools, in Argentina, Australia, Canada, Colombia, Dominican Republic, Germany, Ghana, Guyana, Jamaica, Mexico, South Africa, Spain, and the United Kingdom—a total of seventeen in mid-2005.

Early into 2005 C.E., the Unity Movement has approximately 1,020 ministries in 42 countries with correspondents (potential for more ministries) in 169 countries. For example, from June 2001 to June 2002, we added 22 new ministries, 8 full-service churches, 12 alternative ministries, and 117 informal study groups (first step to becoming a full-fledged ministry). We envision together continuing growth in all nations as we jointly create national schools, thereby making leadership training more accessible and more affordable.

The potential of countries as well as of people provides tremendous outward pressure to share their rich heritage/tradition of the past and of their future potential. Not only is the Association of Unity Churches, International not an institutional monolith, neither is Unity's message a monolith. What gives birth to expressions of Truth is the personal quest for two items: 1) understanding answers to ultimate meaning, and 2) relationships to the world and to the Transcendent, both inherent and "out-there-ent." People the world over have been, and are, giving birth essentially to the same belief systems that Unity and all New Thought movements hold as dear. They have called it by various names—and sometimes they just hold it in their hearts, without names.

Perhaps you will recall the movie *Groundhog Day*. Doesn't progress often feel like that? No matter how much progress appears to be made, it often feels as though we get pulled back to "Go" the next day, which also somehow feels "normal." A desire to change, or for major transformation, is often accompanied by a pulling and tugging by our own known "present behavior" with a desire not to change. We experience both the comfort of the known way, and the discomfort or fear of the unknown. That's part of our continuing motivation for the joint search for spiritual truth by modern science and world religion.

The Joint Search for Spiritual Truth by Modern Science and World Religion 4

The Changing Faces of Reality

KING DAVID, THE PSALMIST, as he reflected on his life and watched the moon and stars move across the dark sky while tending his sheep, tells us, "The Heavens declare the glory of God" (Ps. 19:1). Van Leeuwenhoek clapped his hand to his mouth in awe when he first observed through his microscope a tiny "animal," never before seen by human eyes. And after formulating his groundbreaking equations for general relativity and gravitation, Einstein is said to have made the often-quoted remark, "The most incomprehensible thing about the universe is that it is comprehensible."

Scientists and theologians experience a similar kind of awe and mystery about nature or creation. Although they study the "mysteries" with different methods and for different purposes, could there be an acutely meaningful relationship between science and religion? In some ways, the tremendous technological advances within recent decades have given expanded meaning to our scientific culture. However, for many people, there still remains a strong, inner yearning for greater meaning to life. We search for a significant and purposeful explanation for the questions "What is it all about?" "Who are we?" and "Why are we here?"

If we look through the eyes of scientists, perhaps we see ourselves standing at a midpoint between the infinitely large cosmic space and the infinitesimally small atomic nuclei. If we gaze through the eyes of the philosophers and the theologians, we see ourselves standing midway between the finite and the infinite. From the perspectives of the historians and the archaeologists, we stand between the eternity of the past and the eternity of the future. What important facts and features have we discovered through our inner and outer searching? How do we chart a course for the journey ahead?

In the present time, more people seem moved to search deeply for a greater understanding of the ways of God and the interaction of a "Grand Cosmic Creator" with all of creation. Sir John Templeton wrote, "The manifold scientific discoveries of the late twentieth century cause the visible and tangible to appear less and less real and point to a greater reality in the ongoing and accelerating creative process within the enormity of the vast unseen."[1]

As our ever-more complex world converges on a globally standard material culture built on scientific technology, questions often arise regarding the significance of religious and moral traditions. The astonishing variables reported by anthropological studies challenge us to reappraise the meaning of being human. Interesting questions are being asked with regard to science and religion. How much of the body of knowledge embraced by cosmogony, cosmography, cosmic evolution, and astronomy has been provided by religion and how much by science? On the other hand, how much transcendent reality has the religious (or spiritual) quest for meaning and purpose brought to every culture and every age since the emergence of humankind?

Vast changes have occurred within recent decades to our understanding of physical reality as approached through science. Major changes are also being experienced regarding our understanding of the reality of God that religion provides and theology interprets.

Some Models for Relating Science and Religion

Physicist and theologian Ian Barbour, recent prestigious Templeton Prize winner for his work regarding science and religion, elaborated on several broad categories, or models, he had previously defined for relating science and religion: conflict, independence, dialogue, and integration.[2] We get an understanding of *conflict* between science and religion when we remember Galileo's clash with the church regarding his view of the solar system. History shows that many of the scientists who paved the way for the "scientific age," for example, Boyle, Copernicus, Kepler, Maxwell, and Newton, held close personal beliefs in the God of Scriptures and in prayer.

Following the conflict surrounding Darwin, many scientists and theologians developed an "independent" way of thinking, assuming that science and religion represent independent fields of study. Science has very little to say about religious beliefs, and religion has very little to say about scientific study. This model appeals to both scientists and theologians because it allows them freedom to think and believe what they wish in their respective fields, without having to relate one to the other.

Barbour's *dialogue* model looks for methodological parallels between science and religion. Some scholars support this model because they realize that scientific study is perhaps not as objective as once thought. Both science and religion involve a set of beliefs and a multilevel approach to reality. Barbour then goes a step further by applying scientific methods and standards to religious beliefs and practices.

The *integration* model of relating science and theology is sometimes called the "mutual support" model. Recently, a group of American scientists, including William Dembski, considered natural theology in terms of "Intelligent Design." While accepting all the evidence in support of an ancient universe and most of the evidence for the evolutionary history of life, they argue that there may be an "irreducible complexity" to life that transcends the laws of chance and physics. Others, such as astronomer Howard van Till, and theologian-biochemist Sir Arthur Peacocke, feel that the very laws of science were the methods God used to develop the great variety of living things that exist.

Both scientific and theological expressions of reality use models and metaphors to deal with the complexity and limited precision of their fields. Sometimes I feel almost schizophrenic about science and religion. I cannot tell where one begins and the other leaves off, nor do I wish to try. Continuing to ask the questions of "how" and "why" may provide an avenue to bring science and religion together as joint participants in understanding what Einstein called "the inner justification of natural law."

Perhaps one of Albert Einstein's more familiar statements of his beliefs is: "I believe in Spinoza's God who reveals Himself in the orderly harmony of what exists, not in a God who concerns Himself with fates and actions of human beings."[3] Years later, he expanded on this statement in a letter to Maurice Solovine, the survivor of the Olympia Academy, by writing,

I can understand your aversion to the use of "religion" to describe an emotional and psychological attitude which shows itself most clearly in Spinoza. [But] I have not found a better expression than "religious" for the trust in the rational nature of reality that is, at least to a certain extent, accessible to human reason.[4]

Einstein, as a scientist and philosopher, displayed an especially sensitive attitude toward the religious experience:

The most beautiful and most profound emotion we can experience is the sensation of the mystical. It is the sower of all true science. He to whom this emotion is a stranger, who can no longer wonder and stand rapt in awe, is as good as dead. To know that what is impenetrable to us really exists, manifesting itself as the Highest wisdom and the most radiant beauty which our dull faculties can comprehend only in their most primitive forms—this knowledge, this feeling is at the center of true religiousness.[5]

The sincere seeker after truth in either science or religion cannot afford to ignore the realities both areas can provide. In our search for truth/reality, by whatever name we call the inner longing, it is important to remember the search may sometimes be extremely different, but it is greatly enhanced by realizing the interconnectedness of life and knowledge. Dr. Franklin Loehr, director of research at the Religious Research Foundation of America, Inc. once said,

A single new insight, a key discovery, a different way of looking at things can change the course of Man's understanding. . . . Science as a way of getting information and religion as a field of knowledge to be scientifically explored may prove equally seminal. The development of religion as a science opens a most positive reconciliation of the long-troubled relation of Science and Religion.[6]

Finally, Dr. Billie Grassie, CEO of the Metanexus Institute, wrote,

Religion and science represent two types of humanity's fundamental experience. Wherever there is unity between religion and science, it is more expedient to pay heed to religion [as] it is abundantly richer. When they are in discord, it is better to turn to science as it is more reliable.[7]

The Development of Religion as a Science

Our questions about "ultimate" reality, purpose, and meaning may be searching, exploratory, tentative, and often profound. In the process of our quest for spiritual truth, we seek release from our prejudices and judgments, whether of a philosophical, religious, or scientific nature, and open our minds to the great plan of humanity's purpose of which we are a part. In a vast and intricate cosmos, there is much more to be discovered in unlimited areas and on multitudinous levels. To enjoy the fruits of our discoveries, it seems important to educate and nourish our spirits as well as our minds and bodies.

Working closely with scientists, theologians, medical professionals, philosophers, and other scholars, the John Templeton Foundation encourages substantive dialogue in order to stimulate research and reflection in the relationship between science and religion. The Foundation especially seeks to stimulate rigorous scholarly/scientific advances that increase understanding of the ultimate aspects of human purpose, and of the vast potential for creativity and progress, that can be inspired by the collaboration of science and religion. In pursuing research at the boundary between science and religion, the Foundation seeks to unite credible and rigorous science with the exploration of humanity's basic spiritual and religious quests.

Spiritual studies can inspire reverence, wonder, and awe, and can pose urgent questions of meaning and purpose, of virtues and values. Science can provide insights into the nature of reality across a wide range of domains. Scientific discoveries have often changed both our world and our worldviews. Could the present time in human history be "ripe" for the development of religion as an aspect of science? How might this be accomplished? Has the process already begun? What are some ways that the development of religion as a science may possibly effect changes in the world?

Walter R. Hearn wrote, "Some people today are convinced that a religious view of the world is inherently false, untrustworthy, or at least inferior to a scientific view. Others believe that for a religious view to have credence, it must sound like or be attuned to the most up-to-date scientific description of the world."[8] Religion offers a whole new realm to be scientifically explored. The spiritual dimension offers promise of an exponential expansion of knowledge. The vast physical universe may have "boundaries." But who knows what mysteries await research in the spiritual dimension! Is it possible that there are realms of being beyond realms of being and plane of expression upon plane of expression within the various realms?

Education to gain knowledge of spiritual truth principles is as vitally important as is spiritual practice to prepare the spirit, mind, body for its role in divine selfhood. We can discipline the mind through right thinking, use affirmations and denials, prayer, spiritual mind treatment, meditation (or going into the silence), acts of forgiveness, and focusing on the present moment, exercising either divine or agape love.

Our cumulative knowledge has changed dramatically just within the past fifty years and the pace of accumulation of new data has quickened immensely. How will educators and educational processes—religious, scientific, and secular—keep pace with this explosion during this century, at the beginning of the third millennium? There could be a billion more people to educate in a variety of fields. Considering the pace at which human knowledge is accelerating, especially in the fields of science and technology, what might we anticipate in the more controversial areas of social, religious, and political theories?

Personal experience is often considered by many people to be a powerful "educator" and a convincing way to discover a truth. Yet, seldom do any two persons experience the same thing in the same way. The personal experience is *subjective*, although we can learn to observe objectively and report and evaluate events. Science, on the other hand, seeks the *objective* facts. Science works toward being factually definitive about the subject it researches. It often shows us the hard core of impersonal truth in a given reality.

We in the twenty-first century are blessed to experience two ways of knowing that focus on the search for truth—science and religion—that revere truth above human assumptions or proclamations. Could scientific research eventually discover that there is a "Creator"? Are we poised on a vast spiritual frontier, ready for the brilliant researchers of science to enter these opening doors and explore and discover other dimensions and realms of reality?

Astronomer Allan Sandage spoke of God in terms of the marvelous laws of nature, and Sir Arthur Eddington wrote of a spiritual world that lies behind the universe we study. Teilhard de Chardin, in *The Phenomenon of Man*, told us that knowledge is basic and enables us to understand the world and ourselves and to exercise some control or guidance over our actions.[9] A distillation of Chardin's work seems to indicate that humankind contains the possibilities of the earth's immense future. We can realize more of these wondrous possibilities as we increase our knowledge and ability for universal love. Is it time for a rebirth of images concerning the nature of God as Creator, the act of creation, and the continuing nature of God's creative interaction with the world? How could this greater search for meaning come about? We can look into the labyrinthine architecture of a cell, examine the numbing diversity of the rain forest, and plumb the unfathomable depths of the human brain. We can explore the depths of space and discover heretofore unknown planets, even universes!

Some tremendous "eye-openers" have resulted from the missions operations of the Hubble space telescope. Its numerous highlights include: the Hubble Deep Fields, proof that quasars reside in galaxies, expansion of the universe measured, and proof that gamma-ray bursts are found in galaxies. One recent media press release announced, "Hubble Uncovers a Baby Galaxy in a Grown-up Universe."[10] The news release is electrifying with possibilities!

Our human role in evolving our future and the vast wilderness of unexplored reality is critical. It is important to release the close-minded attitude that says, "I already know it all." The emerging field of cosmology reveals the universe to be larger, by many orders of magnitude, than previously thought. Our scientists research the natural wonders of the universe, devise new hypotheses, test them, challenge old assumptions, and compete with each other. Some religious leaders, theologians, and laypeople do not yet realize that spiritual reality can be researched in ways similar to those used by natural scientists.

The past few decades, with its fascinating discoveries, have influenced many scientists to a sense of awe and, for some, a new and compelling sense of humility. Could the stage be set now for new dialogue between scientists, philosophers, and theologians? Are we on the verge of a grand opportunity for the revitalization of religion, theology, and science departments? What steps might be taken toward the development of religion as a science?

Science and Religion: Partners in Discovery?

The scientist, the philosopher, the poet, and the priest, each in their unique and purposeful ways, bear witness to the evidence of orderliness, the farsightedness, and the wit of the cosmos. It would seem logical that a discussion of humanity's religious future could be set in the context of the present scientific age. One amazing happening is that scientists are beginning to ask "religious" questions. These questions are stimulated by the vastness and the intricacy of the physical world that literally shouts for some kind of explanation regarding design and purpose.

In an article in *Zygon*, Ralph Wendell Burhoe wrote:

> It is my view that the sciences add more than vital new evidence for the credibility of the essential wisdom of ancient theologies in recognizing the reality of a system of superhuman power that created, sustains, and selects us according to how well we meet its requirements for human life and advancement. The sciences also add far clearer evidence than we have had previously that the essential reality of evolving human life included much more than our bodies: something as "inner" to us as our genes and innermost "feelings" and also something as lasting as immortal souls.[11]

Bringing scientists and theologians together within the framework of exploration may be a source of tremendous opportunity for extending our understanding of ourselves and of the spiritual dimension.

In truth, could there really be a conflict between true science and true religion, because they both describe a form of reality? Science is a fact of modern life. Religion is a traditional carrier of meaning. Faith traditions believe in sacred reality, but how does this relate to day-to-day unfolding reality? Could both science and religion provide an important meeting ground for this question? Science and religion serve different roles in human life. At a meeting of the newly formed International Society of Science and Religion (ISSR) in Granada, Spain, Ian Barbour stated, "Science and theology serve different roles in human life. Encouraging dialogue doesn't mean that they are the same, but that they can fruitfully engage."[12]

An exciting aspect of the ISSR is that its members are premier scientists and theologians who know that we have to go beyond our own fields to reach deeper insights. Hopefully, the religious perspectives represented by the ISSR will be beneficial in understanding the world, and competitive in understanding reality. Friendly competition often produces mutual learning and disagreements can usually point the way toward deeper understanding. People have a hunger for knowledge of ultimates, and science and spirituality are two main paths often traversed in trying to glean that knowledge. Surely, the culture of our world is impoverished if scientists and theologians are not encouraged to talk. This is especially vital at this uniquely perilous moment in the planet's natural progression.

Research on Prayer and Its Healing Modalities

In the book *The Power of Prayer*, Joanna Hill and I present some results emerging from research done with regard to prayer.[13] Several projects are mentioned. F. C. Byrd conducted a study in 1988 that tested the therapeutic effect of intercessory prayer on heart patients in San Francisco. Half of the almost four hundred patients were randomly selected to be prayed for by Christian volunteers. These patients were studied for more than ten months and their cases were then analyzed in twenty-six categories. Among these categories were the occurrence of pulmonary edema, the need for intubation (use of a breathing tube), and other measures of health benefits. The research concluded that in twenty-one of the twenty-six categories, the patients who were recipients of prayer fared significantly better. For all patients, prayer was used in addition to standard medical care.

A study conducted by Harold Koenig at Duke University Medical Center found that elderly patients who pray regularly are healthier and happier than those who do not. They found that prayer and meditation reduce stress and thus can dampen the body's production of stress hormones such as adrenaline. For more than thirty years, laboratories at the Harvard Medical School have systematically studied the benefits of mind/body interactions. The research established that when a person engages in a repetitive prayer, word, sound, or phrase and when intrusive thoughts are passively disregarded, a specific set of physiological changes ensues. Metabolism, heart rate, and rate of breathing all decrease, and brain waves slow. The efficacy of prayer can be tested and confirmed.

Pathways Toward Heaven on Earth

Is not each precious individual desirous, on some level, of awakening to greater spiritual consciousness? Do not many of us seek to be a constructive participant in building "heaven on earth" as we live, move, and work in a world that sometimes seems filled with conflict and strife? It is becoming clear that we can create a more loving, peaceful, useful, personal, and universal world by our thoughts, feelings, words, actions, consciousness, and awareness of global positioning for the soul.

How can we transcend the perimeters of seemingly "ordinary" consciousness to soar with the "eagles" of spiritual awareness? Can we begin transforming ourselves through recognition and effective utilization of the power of our mind? Can transformation be effected through spiritual beliefs and practices? Is a radical change possible for individuals through intellectual, emotional, psychological, scientific, spiritual, religious, and/or ritualistic pursuits? How may we comprehend the difference between an intellectual comprehension/understanding and the reality of living action? Can we be objectively self-observant without self-criticism or judgment? As we develop ourselves spiritually and experience the indwelling presence of God, and as we live in accord with universal laws and divine principles, we invariably become more successful in all aspects of human endeavors. Our own creativity can be helpful in finding useful approaches to greater spiritual understanding.

Perhaps you will be inspired to further research and explore deeper aspects of both the *subjective* and *objective* aspects of your personal world. These personal explorations may bring an increasing awareness of the interconnectedness of humanity along with the partnership of science and religion. Although we may seem to live individualistic lives, the expanding divine idea of oneness and unity may be influencing a revolution in consciousness that could transform our world in presently unimaginable ways. Avenues are open to examine the wondrous spiritual nature of humans and, indeed, extensive research and examinations of scientific and religious variables are underway.

The Gifford Lectures

Some of the world's foremost thinking in natural theology is now available in an easily accessible repository. The Gifford Lectures online database, www.giffordlectures.org, was formally launched by Templeton Foundation Press during the Edinburgh Book Festival on August 15, 2005. The site contains the complete text of 48 of the 208 volumes that have currently resulted from the Gifford lectures; one-third of the summaries of those 208 books; and almost half of the biographies of the 212 lectures.

The Gifford Lectures were established by bequest of the jurist Adam Lord Gifford (1820–87) and delivered at the Universities of Edinburgh, Glasgow, Aberdeen, and St. Andrews almost every year since 1888. The lectures were established to address questions related to natural theology, that is, understanding God by light of reason rather than revelation, and have been given by scholars, writers, and scientists with diverse perspectives and intellectual interests. Among the renowned lecturers are William James, John Dewey, Albert Schweitzer, Karl Barth, and Stanley Jaki.

The plan is to continually update the site with the addition of all publications that result from future Gifford lectures.

Helping the World's Great Religions Grow   5

When we embrace the possibility of agape love, we are expressing a unity of purpose, a common hope for all people. It is our opportunity to express God's love radiating through us to others. Unconditional, unlimited, altruistic love holds within it the opportunity to transcend the obvious differences of religious beliefs and live a joyful life in a peaceful world." —Sir John Templeton, Agape Love

A S A SOCIAL PSYCHOLOGIST, I define *religion* not only as Judeo-Christian-Islam monotheism, but also as behaviors deriving from a set of rules and beliefs concerning a universe beyond the visible. Therefore, I include not just God in the definition, but spirits, universal life forces, sun and moon, gods and goddesses, and ancestors.

In most highly organized religions, however devout a true believer may be, the forums of science and/or philosophy allow a kind of escape from the dogmatism of one's religion. Both the scientist and the theologian live in most people, whether professional or lay in either or both fields. Religion satisfies some of the deeper inner longings for peace and a sense of mystery and awe, and of oneness with God or gods, while science satisfies a deep inner need to push the envelope toward intellectual understanding. Each is useful on its own and may be mutually beneficial.

Varadaraja Raman paraphrased a prior statement about Hinduism this way: "[A] Hindu can claim that one is most a Hindu when least a Hindu, i.e., when one has dissolved one's Hindu particularity in Hinduism's all-embracing inclusiveness," reflecting a worldview we may all profitably emulate.[1] The same can be said of Islam, Judaism, Christianity, Buddhism, New Thought, Taoism, Confucianism, or Native American spirituality, and, I hope, the philosophy and history that stand with each of the scientific disciplines.

With this frame of reference in mind, let us look at ways I believe all religious traditions can embrace spiritual seekers globally and welcome them into our houses of worship, fostering involvement that will benefit them individually and as communities, as well as our ministries and the world at large. Communities of believers across the spectrum of the world's great religions may be the hope for ultimate peace and mutual understanding.

Much of the future of the world's great religions may take fifty years to evolve, but what has happened in recent years, what is in process currently, and what is going to happen in this twenty-first century (namely, by 2075 C.E.) is outlined below. Some cultures may change sooner; others will take longer.

1. *Ministry by laity will be the norm, not the exception.*

This will occur in local houses of worship and throughout our organizational structures. Ministry by laity will help large houses of worship grow, especially in large cities, and larger houses of worship than the norm in small cities or communities. Regardless of size, they will increase in effectiveness. More than half will still have fewer than 100 in worship-service attendance, but more than one-third will have more than 1,000 attendees, with several having 1,500 and above in attendance. Staff will include one full-time professional clergy for every 500–800 people at worship, with most of the program staff being lay specialists, full-time, part-time, and many volunteer congregations of 2,000 will regularly have 500–800. Larger congregations will offer a denominational day school from nursery classes through at least grade five. This service to the larger community surrounding our houses of worship becomes more critical each year, given both the unresponsiveness of mass media to the needs of children (and their families) to not be bombarded with violence and atrocities, as well as the increasing ineffectiveness of our public school systems.

2. *The importance of community will be recognized.*

Historically, people have been drawn to our houses of worship because of their teachings. More and more people now seem to be attending their chosen house of worship because of a desire for "relationships" in addition to the teachings. By 2015 C.E., for at least half of worshippers, the majority of friends in their social network will come from among fellow worshippers. With divorce and single parenthood still a major fact through the next few decades for most cultures, religions need to be mindful in preparing both adult and childhood curriculum, as well as activities designed to draw them into the circles (all age levels of the family) of fellowship. Views on sexual orientation are changing in many religions as well.

3. *The way our houses of worship are structured will change.*

Members will give up "administrivia" and professional clergy will give up ministry. Devotees will no longer be on "committees." They will instead be enrolled in *ministry,* such as the hospitality ministry, including, but not limited to, ushers and host(esses), the visitation or chaplaincy ministry, the prayer ministry, or the parish nurse ministry.

These ministries are the beginnings of what I call "ministries within ministries," "nurture ministry," or "nurture groups." Clergy will still be necessary for teaching, but a greater portion of their time will involve recruiting, capacity-building (training), and nurturing devotees to perform ministry. We will look for "yes" answers to the three sociological questions: a) Can I get in? b) Will I be accepted? and c) Can I make a difference? In fact, these questions will increasingly serve as a guide to people as to whether they want to be a part of a given religious community.

4. *New definitions of authentic spirituality will be created.*

It won't be defined by reading the Bible, Torah, Bhagavad Gita, Koran or other sacred documents or teaching or attending adult or children's classes. This one is akin to number 2 above. Authentic spirituality will address first the taking in of spiritual literature and meditation and then will address: "How can I use what I've absorbed and truly serve in relationship to those in my religious/spiritual community and then to my larger community of humankind?" With new "ears" we will hear Spirit tell us to heal one person and "carry water" for another. The continuing growth in our houses of worship in part will be because of people's driving proclivity for holistic healing and wellness programs. They are interested in meditation, prayer, nutrition, homeopathy, and the mind/body connection. As they learn, they will then want to "pass it on" through service. Over the doors where people enter our worship services we might place a sign that says, "Enter to worship," and over the doors where they leave, perhaps a sign that says, "Exit to serve." Inside those doors, much of the worship is also service to fellow worshippers. These messages might be placed on signs at drive entrances and exits as well.

5. Those with no religious affiliation will be reached

Our missions are in our own backyards and in our houses of worship. We are "disciples" (students) of our own belief system and then we become "apostles" (teachers), but since there is no culture in the world without religion and/or spirituality, we increasingly will mean it when we say there are many paths to God. All those who wish to come will be welcome, just as they are now, but there will be an increased emphasis on reaching those with no religious affiliation. (In the coming years, there will be a precious few, if any, who have no spiritual inclinations, whether they have a religious affiliation or not.)

The five points above speak of pervasive, deep-tissue change. Over the next twenty years, changes and "transitions" will occur rapidly. An operational "distinction" between the terms can be seen in the following anecdote. As you drive your car, a tire is destroyed. The tire must be changed. With no one else to change the tire for you, you change it yourself. That's "change."

The "transition" and all the resistance and "talking" to the tire about what a bad time it is to have a flat (as though there was a good time) from the time the tire blows out until the change is complete and you're on the road again can represent a process of transition. Transitioning can also go on much longer—all the way from replacing the damaged tire to paying for it a month or so later. And, of course, the road is smoother as our perceptions are made finer; we draw the beginning and the ending of both changes and transitions closer together, whether on the highway or on one's spiritual journey.

An observation: One morning, a friend was driving me to be the guest speaker at her church. On the highway, we passed about twelve to fifteen eighteen-wheeler trucks, all from the same company, each with the logo "Delivering your future." My guess is that some people may believe that their future *is* being delivered by a truck!

But it is not. Our future is being delivered both by the "collective unconscious" and by our conscious choices. Some of the conscious choices we can make regarding increasing the numbers as well as deepening our experiences with people follow.

Making First-Timers Feel Welcome

First, take care not to refer to guests in a house of worship as "visitors." Instead, during the service, we need to ask, "Will all those who are with us for the first time today please stand so that we can welcome you?" Thereafter, refer to them as "first-timers." This leads easily to encouraging that there be a "second time." "Visitors" on the other hand, are not expected to return. After all, they are "only visiting."

Once the first-timers can be identified after the service by carrying a "Welcome" envelope or wearing a ribbon or name tag, hospitality "ministry" team members (often erroneously referred to as "hospitality committee"), also wearing name tags, need to proactively engage the first-timer(s). Invite them, and accompany them, to the fellowship area if that is traditional, introduce them to the clergy and other leaders who are available, and to at least two other people before they leave.

Many clergy use the twenty-four- or thirty-six-hour rule; that is, either they or an assignee (hospitality or visitation ministry team member, or chaplain) call by phone or use any other available and acceptable means of communication within a culture to repeat the welcome within thirty-six hours at the outside.[2] That is a good place to begin and there is no reason not to maximize the value of that call by taking a brief survey in addition to extending a welcome. (The "first-timer" will also receive a letter signed by the clergy within a week of the first visit to the house of worship and a second call by the eighth day after attendance.)

The size of the ministry may determine whether it is the clergy or an assignee who calls. It is vital for the clergy to make the calls personally until mounting responsibilities disallow it. From here on, I shall refer to the clergy or assignee simply as the "caller" and the worship guest as the "first-timer." The term *newcomer* is appropriate only after the third or more times of joining in worship. Prior to that time, the first- or second-timer may consider being called a newcomer "presumptive."

The caller begins by asking if the first-timer has five minutes (more if absolutely necessary, but be specific and brief) to answer six questions (add to or delete from a number of questions, but be specific and brief) that will help our religious/spiritual community do a better job of welcoming first-timers. Once first-timers know who is calling, most are willing to help.

The rationale for the questions follows the list of questions.

1. Tell me please, why did you attend our (church, synagogue, mosque, temple, etc.)?

2. Please tell me how you first found out about our religious/spiritual community.

3. Please tell me what you liked about our house of worship when you attended.

4. What didn't you like?

5. On a continuum segmented from one to ten with ten being highest, how warmly greeted did you feel when you attended?

6. Can you tell me what you are looking for in a spiritual home?

If for any reason the call is made a week later and the first-timer has become a second-timer, a seventh question might be, "Why did you come back?"

Clergy Survey Calls

This call provides a good first contact (or second, if the caller has already visited the first-timer in person). Whether the clergy makes the survey call or not, if at all possible, it may be helpful if she/he calls within ten days from the first time of attending. In the past, many clergy have tended to avoid these procedures, thinking that they "smack" of emotional "arm twisting," or that the procedures are too time-consuming. Probably many professional or lay leaders who do not visit or call do not because of personal discomfort. Seen from the first-timer's viewpoint, however, this contact is more often viewed as caring, and the first-timer feels it. He/she needs to know someone wants to let them into the "community circle."[3]

The survey provides an opportunity for a personal conversation that probably was not possible at the close of worship. The survey questions usually generate other conversation in which the caller gets acquainted with the first-timer and his/her needs.

Quite likely, the basic reason the caller doesn't more commonly perform the above behaviors is the personal discomfort of just calling or visiting to "see how you're doing." The survey does two things:

It provides legitimate research that possibly/probably will change or continue to update the greeting of new worshipers.

The survey provides an easy entrance into the possibility of an otherwise awkward conversation (bearing in mind that well over 50 percent of all religious professionals are introverts).

The survey conveys an important message: "You are important to us; we care what you think; we would like you to return to worship with us." As we are increasingly learning, much of fundraising is "asking"; so is membership and/or prospective participant assimilation largely "asking."

Finally, the survey as an entrance to talking allows the first-timer to ask about our spiritual community—especially when we tell the first-timer, "In exchange for responding to my questions, you can ask me anything you like." People who are looking are likely to ask some really good questions. And we are likely to learn some really good answers to our questions of them.

For clergy and friends and members of every congregation: "Describe a person to whom you not only would, but do, make to feel welcome his/her first time to your house of worship." Periodically, I ask clergy and friends and members of every congregation to do just that. The answers are wide-ranging, often including the statement that "We welcome everybody!" In asking a few more questions, we often discover that the descriptions given are of people who already attend. But even that is not a complete answer. The exercise is to describe a person whom you make to feel welcome when he/she *first* attends. One of the reasons I often include this exercise is because of an experience I had in a ministry that I served that showed me we were practicing discrimination "unawares." One of my practices systematically in attempting to assimilate newcomers over the years was to interview each new person personally, accompanied by at least one volunteer department leader from the major "ministries" (or departments) of our church. The idea was manifold: it allowed the new person to become acquainted with about a dozen ministry leaders and what they did in the church, it also allowed those dozen volunteers and me to become better acquainted with the newcomer, and it encouraged the newcomer to look at how he/she might want to become involved.

Later, I would ask for a follow-up interview with me alone. In one such procedure a woman told me what a joyous, enthusiastic, welcoming feeling she received from the congregation and the new members' support ministry. A few days later, a man who attended the same introductory class as the woman told me what a "cold fish" congregation and support ministry we had. He felt very unwelcome and said if it were not for the message that he had by now learned he needed and wanted so much, he would have already left membership. These two friends were reporting on the same congregation and, largely, on the same support ministry members.

One of two variables can be addressed: both individuals were of the same race as most of the congregation and most of the ministry members. The congregation and support ministry members were close to 50-50 in men and women. The woman felt welcomed by men and women; the man felt not welcomed by men and women.

Differences? Yes. The woman was upwardly mobile, educated, articulate, and finely groomed and dressed. The man may not have finished high school; he was struggling financially and, therefore, was not well dressed.

Welcoming only those who look like us, talk like us, and so on eventually will make us extremely segregated. The greater the variety we attract, the greater opportunity we have to reach out to the myriad people who are looking for a spiritual community of which to become a real part.

The following brief list can be expanded *ad infinitum*. Make copies and give two copies to at least key volunteers, including those who work with new members, to rank order two different ways. First, they should rank order for themselves, 1) a top-priority person to welcome, 2) a medium-priority person to welcome, and 3) those least likely to receive much (if any) efforts in welcoming. Then, on their second list, ask them to provide the same ranking of how, based on their observations of members and attendees, they think others might function regarding welcoming.

After asking participants to decide who would receive welcome easily, not so easily, and probably not at all, bring them together to see if a consensus can be drawn. Likely, for some groups from descriptions above, number 1 will be easy to agree upon. Go on to number 2, or "medium" group. Begin with at least three to five descriptions to see if, with a little work and effort, your leaders might be led to plan strategies for welcoming the medium category into your church. Perhaps this is where the greatest outreach can take place with the number 3 group. It is not the "not-so-welcome" category, but we might all be surprised how much folks in this group are willing and able to give back in talents, presence, and love. It takes intentional effort and planning on the part of the leadership as a whole to make our houses of worship inviting and inclusive.

WHO IS TRULY WELCOME?
DO OUR WORDS AND BEHAVIOR MATCH?

An extremely obese male

An extremely obese female

Divorced male

Divorced female

Aging male with financial resources

Aging female with financial resources

Ex-convict

Lower-income male

Lower-income female

HIV-positive person

Middle-class male

Middle-class female

Gay male

Lesbian female

Male of another ethnic group

Female of another ethnic group

A gay couple

A lesbian couple

Someone shy and retiring

Person with alcohol on his/her breath

Severely physically disabled person

Someone especially talkative

Single male under 30

Unmarried pregnant teenager

Person on welfare

Smoker

Alzheimer's patient

Male with nontraditional ("inappropriate") apparel

Female with nontraditional ("inappropriate") apparel

Person with noticeable hygiene problem

Articulate, well-educated, well-to-do male of another ethnic origin

Articulate, well-educated, well-to-do female of another ethnic origin

Retarded youth or child

Emotionally disturbed person with unpredictable behavior

Questions of First-Time Worshippers

"Can I get in? Will I be accepted? Can I make an impact?" are the first three questions first-timers to a worship service have.[4] They need to hear, to see, and to experience that the answer is "Yes!"

The "revolving-door syndrome" (sometimes called "in the front door and out the back" syndrome) is probably something it is not possible to stop completely. It is safe to say that at least a few of our first-timers are not "ready" and do not return for years, if ever. Much as I would have preferred not to face it when I was previously in leadership in a house of worship, I think it is also safe to say some (perhaps many) of our first-timers were ahead of me and my message and they did not return for years, if ever. Even then, perhaps their return was to see if I had yet "caught up," and, therefore, might have something useful for them to hear.

Acknowledging the risk I've taken above at simplifying the two ends of the "spiritual-home shopper" continuum, what about all the people in between? It takes more than a well-constructed and well-delivered lesson and it takes more than a moving program of music or other worship component to a perfectly executed service to get those first-timers to become second-timers and beyond. We also cannot just rely on cultural affinity to cause first-timers to become second-timers.

It also takes more than a tongue-in-cheek publishing of the following suggestions, along with their accompanying statistics: "Do not ride in automobiles; they cause 20 percent of all fatal accidents. Do not stay at home; 17 percent of all accidents occur in the home. Do not walk on the street or sidewalk; 14 percent of all accidents occur to pedestrians. Do not travel by air, rail, or water; 16 percent of all accidents happen on these. However, only .001 percent of all deaths reported occur in worship services. Hence, the safest place for you to be is in a house of worship. Youth activities are also relatively safe."

What does it take to get first- and second-timers and newcomers (people who have returned after their second time) to return? For starters, it takes desire on the part of the professional and lay leadership to have them return.

Fostering inclusion is not automatic in the small house of worship any more than it is in the mid-sized or large ones. Logistically, welcoming and including first-timers, familiarizing newcomers, and assimilating new members could be easier in small houses of worship than in larger, but it still takes desire and well-executed plans to make it happen.

The "small ministry syndrome" is a fact in ministry. Many devotees say they want their house of worship to grow, but they do not mean it. That's true of some clergy, too. It is comfortable to go where "everyone knows my name."

Professional and lay leadership need to recognize and create strategies to transform when possible, and to transcend when necessary, the inertia created by the desire to remain small.

In my experience serving all sizes of houses of worship in various sized cities, it seemed all needed very similar processes for identifying and welcoming first-timers, such as greeting "first-timers" (not "visitors") during announcements and asking them to stand and to receive a packet of information (often with a ribbon or flower to wear), encouraging the newcomer to continue involvement, and finding ways of assimilating new members into ongoing participation.

A small worship center of fifty may well have one first-timer per week (or 52 per year). Using these (or other) proactive assimilation strategies increases the likelihood of getting at least half of them to return regularly or periodically.

Although I encourage reference to first-timers and not "visitors," I am impressed with the practice of some houses of worship that have several greeters trained and experienced at "packet spotting." The first-timer is greeted personally after the service and is not only invited, but escorted to the place of refreshments and fellowship. This one first-timer is the only assignment the greeter has for this day. One portion of the assignment is to be certain that she/he gets a personal introduction to the clergy as well as to others. By design, they are introduced to other greeters and first-timers with the intention of identifying three to five "names with faces." The other greeters are trained to take note of the name and face of each first-timer to whom they are introduced, in the event that the first-timer becomes a "newcomer" in the next few weeks.

At least three or four times a year, a two- to four-week orientation series with refreshments is necessary for newcomers. Depending on the size of the orientation group, you might ask each person to share a little about themselves and what brought them to this house of worship. (Include at least six greeters and other lay leaders and ask them to participate as well.) In a nonthreatening way, they will see commonality not only with other newcomers, but with the leadership as they tell what and how they were led to this house of worship.

In the second session (or second half of the first session if the group is small), since the newcomers have shared a little of their history, share a brief history of the denomination and then a brief history of the local house of worship.

In the third (or second if small) session, clergy and lay leadership share specifics of educational programs, additional worship service information (types of special seasonal or other traditional services), fellowship opportunities, congregational events, information about classes for membership, if required, and service projects. This is where newcomers would tell you their interests and/or skills and what they would like to do. Be sure they list at least three to five volunteer possibilities for "ministry team," not "committee," service. It's a good idea to end this session with dinner (or lunch). This gives newcomers and members further informal opportunity to continue getting acquainted.

The last in the orientation sessions occurs during the following regular worship service. List their names in the program if one is used, introduce them and welcome them, irrespective of whether they plan to become "official" members. This is their day of special honor.

Afterwards, be sure newcomers are recruited to help stage special services, picnics, and any ministry or community service projects.

1. *"Can I get in?"*

Normally, from a physical point of view, the answer is "Yes." (Check and update if necessary the specially-abled physical facilities.)

2. *"Will I be accepted?"*

The answer to this question depends on the desire of the professional and lay leadership and their collective abilities to transform this desire into action on the part of many.

3. *"Can I make an impact?"*

Even the newly attending person who is aware that she/he has such a question usually is hesitant to volunteer. Recruit him or her. Show that he or she can make a difference.

Help the person coming through the front door to hear, to see, and to experience "Yes!" to the three questions above. Most won't look for the back door!

Encourage Friends to Come to Worship Services

Ministry growth specialists tell us that of all the people who first attend any house of worship, 85 percent of those who stay and make it their "spiritual home" were not introduced by any form of advertising, nor by a professional clergy call, but were invited by friends, relatives, or work associates who were already attending that particular house of worship. Assuming the validity of the first statistic, that means that the other 15 percent who stay in their new "spiritual home" first came by all the other means combined.

If we really believe that "an apple a day" will do what we have heard that it will, we would encourage all our friends, family members, and work associates to eat one apple every day just to remain healthy. We are convinced that one must eat food to develop and maintain energy and physical well-being, and if someone close to us did not eat for lack of food, we would do all within our power to see that that person had food to eat in order to sustain a healthy body and a vigorous life.

We know that spiritual nourishment is a "must" in order to sustain a healthy, vigorous, spiritual life. One of the best gifts you can give your friends, loved ones, students, and fellow worshippers is not only permission, but encouragement to invite someone (perhaps several persons) dear to them to attend classes or services with them at their local ministry, or to introduce them to some of the classic readings within their faith.

I believe avoidance of proselytizing is analogous to the person who walks by a burning house in the middle of the night, knowing there are people sleeping inside, but excuses his/her noninvolvement by saying, "Oh, well, when it gets hot enough inside that house, they'll wake up and save themselves."

We are aware of how much our own religious/spiritual foundation enriches our lives to share the message we love so much; we get a firmer grip on our own understanding of our teachings, and those with whom we share receive a "double portion" of our loving, caring, and concern. I repeat the invitation: Give your friends, loved ones, students, and fellow worshippers the gift of encouragement to extend invitations to others to come to worship services, and to introduce them to others' faith literature, traditions, and practices so that they may join in the enriched life that you and I experience as we share our sacred beliefs.

> The rich variety of world religions creates a tapestry of amazing beauty—a testimony to the essential spiritual nature of our human existence. And yet, within this amazing, and sometimes fascinating diversity can be found an equally amazing unity, the basis of which is "love." Perhaps without even being fully aware of it, religious leaders and their followers through the ages have defined religion largely in terms of love. All the world's great religions, to varying degrees, both teach and assume the priority of love in religious practice. —Sir John Templeton, *Agape Love*

The World Parliament of Religions: 6
Barcelona, Spain, July 2004

A Collective Positioning for All Souls of the World

WITH MORE THAN 7,000 ATTENDEES, representing eighty countries and hundreds of denominations, to be sure, there were thousands of views and experiences of the Parliament. Some were experienced in preparation for participation, some gleaned experiences while we were present, and certainly thousands had aftermath experiences. This review is primarily my personal experience and my observations of others' experiences through the eight days (July 7–13, 2004).

'The new and improved version of the World Parliament was a full, empowering, and inspirational experience. This Parliament was very pluralistic. All of the world's major ("major" defined in numbers of adherents only) and hundreds of the minor (again, in numbers of adherents only) religions' representatives were present. The vast majority of Protestant Christian movements were birthed in the United States and even the other major religions are subdivided into "denominations" or sects. More than half of the attendees were from the United States. Most of the denominations are subdivided by gradations of differences. Just as the Unity movement has conservatism and liberalism and all the graduations between, so do Buddhism, Islam, Judaism, and the Catholic Church. We really are very much alike!

As a prelude to the 2004 Parliament, the program began with a brief review of the three previous Parliaments over the previous 111 years and an orientation to the one we were in. The first Parliament in 1893 and the second in 1993 were both held in Chicago. The third was in Capetown, South Africa, in 1999. With the fourth in 2004 (in Barcelona, Spain), they are now intended to occur at five-year intervals. Wherever you are, I encourage you to attend the one in 2009, site yet unknown.

The main contribution of 1893 was that it generated academic interest from East and West in the study of comparative religions. Apparently it also had an indirect effect in prompting the creation of the International Association for Religious Freedom in 1900. However, the Parliament itself was not resurrected until 1993.

In 1993, in Chicago, the assembly was invited to consider the document that came to be known as "Towards a Global Ethic: An Initial Declaration," which presented four ethical principles common across the major Eastern and Western traditions. Since that time, the Declaration has been translated into many languages and has provided the focus of many books and engendered much additional study.

In 1999, the council broadened participation in the Assembly of Leaders to include young people. Gratifyingly, young people were very evident in 2004, as well as leaders from eight guiding institutions: Religion and Spirituality; Government; Agriculture, Labor, Industry, and Commerce; Education; the Arts and Communications Media; Science and Medicine; International Governmental Organizations; and Organizations of Civil Society. These leaders considered another document, "A Call to Our Guiding Institutions," which presented an invitation to people leading these institutions to consider how they would behave if they took seriously the ethical principles from the Global Ethic work of 1993.

One observation I made in comparing my attendance in 1993 and now was that in 1993 I don't remember hearing individuals or representatives of groups making distinctions between spirituality and religion. There were numerous such distinctions made this time. For that matter, most of the scientists I know personally make the same distinction now and probably most did not in 1993.

It is interesting to note that print and oral communications were in three languages: Spanish, Catalan, and English, with multiple language translations.

Committing to Work on Four Major Issues

In July 2004, the Parliament Council invited leaders and activists, experts in critical issues, young people, those impacted by one of four issues, and Parliament participants to develop commitments for their local religious and spiritual communities and institutions.

There was a call for religious and spiritual communities and other institutions to develop and enact practical and transformative, "simple and profound" responses to these four issues:

Improving the plight of refugees.

Relieving the crushing burden of international debt on poor and emerging countries. (Following this intention in 2004, eight of the world's richest nations, the G-8, in July 2005 forgave the indebtedness of the world's fifteen most impoverished nations.)

Creating access to clean water.

Overcoming religiously motivated violence.

The participants at the Parliament were invited to commit and to act. One of the actions was to ask their communities to also commit and act. At the heart of the process, participants and their communities were asked to view the four issues through the lens of their own traditions:

What in your own (and others') tradition compels and inspires you to care about this issue? (You choose which issue.)

How does the strategy for social change embedded in the teachings of your own and others' traditions shape your response?

Please consider this: It is all right for each of us to teach our values and beliefs about religion and politics. To maintain the separation of church and state in the United States of America, clergy are not (although many do) supposed to campaign for political leaders who espouse those same beliefs. (Usually the only trouble clergy get into for doing so is within their own communities, because they run a good chance of offending one-half of their congregations.) However, as a member of an interfaith group, you may have more secular and political clout.

Add the following into the mix of the paragraph above: As a New Thought minister, I have never had the mayor of my city or a representative of city council call me for advice or invite me to come to a meeting for any input I may have. (Occasionally, I have been invited to lead an invocation.) However, as members of an interfaith movement in our cities, we may be either individually or, more likely, collectively with our interfaith group, be asked to participate in a citywide event, or perhaps give input on given issues facing our city. In one of my former ministries, several members and I became known in the city as a mini–United Nations.

If there is an interfaith organization or "initiative" in your city, you may

want to join it and become active if it is active (actually making a difference) in your larger community. If not, you may want to start such an
organization.

For a first-hand account by a Unity colleague on how such a group may
work with a mayor and/or a city council, you may want to call Kyra Baehr
in Chandler, Arizona. She is a part of a "mover and shaker" group called
"The Arizona Interfaith Initiative."

Whether you become active in an existing interfaith organization or
you create one, you may also find the Web site of the International Association for Religious Freedom of great help: www.iarf.net and
www.interfaithalliance.org (a new soon-to-be global network of interfaith).

The Global Positioning of the Soul

Perhaps now is the time for "seven-league strides" in the Unity and all
New Thought movements' transformation and the steady forward progress for all humankind, whether or not they embrace New Thought,
Ancient Wisdom. This is an important time and we are all in the right
place to embrace the soul . . . "Global Positioning of the Soul."

So now, position yourself, no matter your age or place on the planet,
for *your* next steps of Transformation, not your most recent steps, and
not to just repeat your first steps. Rather, when the knock comes to the
door of *your* consciousness and bids you to "come with me," leap into your
next steps!

Preface of the *Metaphysical Bible Dictionary*[1]

T HIS *Metaphysical Bible Dictionary* is offered by the Unity School of Christianity to meet a very definite demand on the part of Bible students and of metaphysicians generally for a work setting forth in simple language the inner, esoteric meanings of scriptural names.

Apart from its being a book of great historical and biographical interest, the Bible is, from Genesis to Revelation, in its inner or spiritual meaning, a record of the experiences and the development of the human soul and of the whole being of man; also it is a treatise on man's relation to God, the Creator and Father. Therefore we are confident that this dictionary will prove very beneficial to Bible students. By opening up new avenues of thought, it will inspire a greater understanding and interest in studying the Scriptures, and will aid its readers much in solving life's problems.

The metaphysical interpretations given in this dictionary are based on the practical teachings of Jesus Christ, as understood and taught by the Unity School of Christianity under the direction of Charles Fillmore and Myrtle Fillmore, its founders. In this dictionary, Mr. Fillmore's interpretations, which have appeared in *Unity* magazine and in other Unity literature from time to time, have been used. The Bible names that had not appeared in the lessons published in Unity literature have been interpreted (with Mr. Fillmore's approval) by Theodosia DeWitt Schobert, who was formerly employed in the Unity Editorial Department and in the Society of Silent Unity.

The names with their pronunciation are taken from Nelson's American Standard Version of the Bible, teacher's edition. Whenever this version gives a spelling different from that set forth in the King James, or Authorized Version, both are given. The American Standard Version spelling is shown first, and is followed by that of the Authorized Version in parentheses, thus: Zerubbabel (A.V., Zorobabel). Following these, the name is syllabified and marked for pronunciation, thus: zē-rüb'-bá-bël. The diacritical marks employed are those used in the American Standard Version. Following the pronunciation of each name, the tongue from which it originated is indicated: (Heb.) for Hebrew, (Aram.) for Aramaic, (Gk.) for Greek, and so on.

In the compilation of the word definitions, which go far in forming the foundations for the metaphysical interpretations, great care has been exercised. Many authorities and lexicons have been consulted in the preparation of this part of the work. Whenever a divergence of opinion between authorities of equal weight was found, the most reasonable etymology was followed.

So far as possible, except where the etymology has become lost, the definitions have been traced back to their original root ideas. These simple ideas, out of which more or less complex expressions have often developed, have been given first; in each case definitions that have developed out of the root idea are given in sequence. This feature is an innovation, and should make for greater clarity in the deeper understanding of the Scriptures.

Many of the Hebrew words that form the basis of proper names derive from pure abstractions, and thus have acceptations that may be either good or bad. Take for instance the word Cain, which comes from the root idea of centralized power, accretion, or accumulation. On the one hand this name could be an expression for benign rulership, kingly qualities, lawful possession, and the like; on the other hand it could stand for despotism, usurpation, extreme selfishness. This peculiarity of the Hebrew tongue has been a source of confusion to many Bible students, and has not been explained in many Bible helps that have been published. This is also a reason for much apparent disparity among the authors of Bible helps wherein only a one-word definition is given: some have taken one acceptation while others have adopted another. In this dictionary the aim has been to clarify. The large number of definitions selected in giving the meaning of names will help the student to feel his way into many bypaths of metaphysical deduction.

One can also gather from the differences and similarities in name definitions something that we have found to be a fact in our experience in studying the Scriptures. This fact is that Scripture names cannot be limited to any one interpretation; no one can truthfully say that a certain text means such or such a thing and nothing else. A dozen persons may get inspiration in a dozen different ways from one Scripture text.

Following the definitions given for each name will be found a brief sketch of the individual, or place, with references telling where the name can be found in the Bible. Unless some particular incident warrants calling attention to it elsewhere, only one reference is given. This reference is either to the place where the name first appears, to that which explains most clearly the historical facts regarding the person or place for whom or which the name stands, or to the passage discussed in the metaphysical interpretation. Wherever the name of an individual is spelled differently in other texts, where another name is used, or where there are several persons bearing the same name, note is made of such fact. In a few cases we have found two names alike, apparently, but separated and having entirely different meanings. This is due to the spelling in translations, which cannot or does not convey the differences in the Hebrew spelling. An instance of this kind is found in Abel, second son of Adam, which should be spelled Hebel, and Abel, the name of several villages. In the Hebrew the two names are spelled with entirely different letters of the alphabet.

Following the biographical sketch of a name comes the metaphysical interpretation. This abbreviation is headed *Meta.*, an abbreviation of "metaphysical." By *metaphysical* we refer to the inner or esoteric meaning of the name defined, as it applies to every unfolding individual and to his relation to God.

We have found in interpreting Bible names that there are varying phases or shades of meaning connected with some of them, beyond that conveyed in the strict definition of the name word. Who the individual was, who his father or mother was, what his occupation was, who his associates were—all these things are modifying factors that we must consider in working out the true character definitions and the metaphysical interpretations as they relate to man generally. Thus we may have two or more men with identical names, each of whom may relate to a different line of thought and develop very different characteristics. These character indexes, which we call names, might therefore be symbolic of diverse phases of Truth or error, and different applications of it. For instance, suppose that we have an Israelite and a Gentile with the same name. The two men would symbolize different planes of consciousness in the individual. The Israelite would relate to the religious tendencies, wither intellectual or spiritual; the Gentile would relate to some phase of the outer man—perhaps to the carnal, sensual, or purely material if he were an enemy of the Israelites.

Furthermore, the social status of the individual whose name is being analyzed and interpreted has to be considered. Whether he was a king, a prince, a priest, a governor, a freeman, or a slave makes a difference in the importance or influence of the idea that he represents. His occupation is also taken into consideration. If he were a shepherd, the significance would differ from what it would be were he a warrior, a hunter, or a tiller of the soil.

The student will find the foregoing methods of analysis worked out in the metaphysical interpretations. We do not wish to convey the impression, however, that the reader will find herein presented the beginning and the end of all Bible symbology and of the phases of Truth that may be developed from it. The interpretations given are suggestions, by no means final. Each may be worked out more fully and comprehensively. An entire volume could easily be devoted to one name, in many cases. If the reader will trust to his own indwelling spirit of truth for light, he will find in these suggestions a guide to endless inspiration in the understanding of Truth.

The Scriptures veil their metaphysical meaning under the names of towns, rivers, seas, and so forth, and the acts of men in connection therewith. The name of each person and of everything in the Scriptures has an inner meaning, a clue to which may be found in any teachers' Bible under such a head as "Names and Their Meanings." For instance, Bethlehem means "house of bread," and indicates the nerve center at the pit of the stomach, through which universal substance joins the refined or spiritualized chemical products of the body metabolism. Through this center are gradually generated the elements that go to make up the spiritualized body of the Christ man. Jesus was born in Bethlehem of Judea.

All is mind, and all material forms are pictures of ideas. By studying a picture we may get a concept of the idea that it represents. The Statue of Liberty at the entrance to New York Harbor, showing the goddess as enlightening the world, is the picture of an idea that nearly everybody understands. It was made by a man as an embodiment of his idea of American freedom and its majesty. Divine Mind has ideas, and they become embodied through natural processes. The Hebrew Scriptures give a series of pictures representing those ideas.

The product of the first day's creation is recorded in Genesis as being "heaven," "earth," and "light." Heaven represents spiritual ideas. Earth represents material thoughts. Light represents understanding.

The firmament in the midst of the waters is an idea of confidence or faith in the invisible. Waters represent changing conditions, which are a necessary part of creation; but when faith establishes itself and separates what is above (spiritual) from what is below (material), the result is harmony or heaven.

The dry land is the thought form, or substance concept, in which the seed of propagation or increase is implanted.

The lights in the firmament, one to rule the day and the other to rule the night, are ideas of intelligent action (lights) in both the conscious and subconscious realms of mind.

The abundant bringing forth of the waters is the fecundity of the mind, which great fishes symbolize. In order to bring forth great results the mind must realize its innate thinking capacity to be great.

After the idea of unlimited capacity follows the image and likeness of God, the ideal or divine man. Then appears the man idea in its developing or evolution phase. As Adam and Eve, the man idea is the innocent child of nature, just entering experience. As Cain and Abel, it is developing the idea of self-preservation from the standpoint of personality. Noah is the thought of obedience and of the safety that follows.

Abraham is a partially developed photograph of the faith idea, which is more fully brought out in Peter. Jacob is the accumulative idea in process of development under divine guidance.

The New Testament is a veiled textbook for the initiate who is seeking degrees in the inner life. It gives rules for working out every mental state that may be found in the mind. It is like a textbook in which are acted out by living figures all the rules for working every problem that may come up in human life.

The key to the mystical theme of the New Testament is found in the spiritual nature of its star character, Jesus Christ. *Christ* is the Greek form of the Hebrew *Messiah*, and the Messiah is the anointed of God, or God identified as perfect man. This perfect man was the image and likeness of Elohim, described in the 1st chapter of Genesis. The perfect man idea or

I AM of Elohim appears in the 2nd chapter of Genesis as Jehovah God, or I AM God. Throughout the Old Testament, up to the advent of Jesus Christ, Jehovah is concerned with the evolution of man. The Christ, or Jehovah, in Jesus affirmed its Mosaic antecedent in the statement, "Before Abraham was born, I am." The Christ claimed also that Moses wrote of Him, again identifying Jehovah and Christ. Jesus represented the external consciousness, or Adam, the man that the Christ or Jehovah formed (in the Edenic allegory) out of the dust of the ground, or elemental substance.

Jesus worked out step by step in His three years' ministry spiritual and mental formulas that we all can apply and thus be healed of our sins and ills of mind and body. By following Him as Guide, Teacher, and Helper we can finally attain the perfect expression of the divine-ideal man imaged by Elohim in the 1st chapter of Genesis. Interpreters of Jesus have given slight value to the part that the body plays in the redemption of man, but Jesus Christ plainly teaches that the whole man—spirit, soul, and body—must be redeemed from the effects of sin. He overcame death and saved His body from the grave. He promised that all those who followed Him in the regeneration would do likewise. Question arises as to how this doctrine was, and is, applied to the restoration of man's body. The various processes in raising the body to wholeness are symbolized in the many healings wrought by Jesus. Every so-called miracle of His points to the transformation of some function of the body consciousness. For example, consider His changing of water to wine at Cana of Galilee. Cana means *"place of reeds"* (the larynx); and Galilee means *"rolling energy, rolling, turning,"* or, as we say in modern terms, "vibration." So we understand that the first miracle of Jesus (the I AM), the turning of water into wine in Cana of Galilee, represents the change that goes on in the waters of life, or the nerve fluids, as they are brought into vibration by a spiritually quickened man or woman. The waters of life are thus changed into wine, or are given elements of greater stimulating, life-giving power than they possessed before they passed through the vibration of the voice. The whole organism may be invigorated and stimulated through the vibratory thrill of the voice. In connection with this miracle there is a still more interior meaning. The six water pots indicate that, when the six great nerve centers in the body are purified, "after the Jews' manner of purifying," the vibratory power of the voice will become so great that by the spoken word a vessel filled with water may be changed into wine. The means by which this purification can be accomplished and the power thus acquired are also explained in the symbolism of the Old Testament.

We could go on thus through all the Bible, but the foregoing is enough to show how we see in the Bible symbolical pictures showing the growth and unfoldment of the latent spiritual power in man up to the time when he comes into manifestation of the perfect "image" and "likeness" in which he was created.

In presenting these methods of interpretation we have endeavored to give with each one sufficient explanation to enable the student to get an idea as to how and why we arrive at given metaphysical conclusions. By reasoning along the same lines the student can develop the inner interpretation of the Scriptures for himself. Our real aim is to assist in leading the student into the inner or spiritual interpretation of the Bible, that he may apply it in the very best and most practical way in his own life. If he does not wish to accept our interpretations, but would rather do his own thinking, entirely apart from our suggestions, we fully recognize his right to do so. We are always pleased when anyone learns to go within and get his inspiration direct from his own indwelling Lord or Spirit of truth. By doing this a person will come to appreciate, as he can in no other way, the patient, faithful effort that culminates in the production of such books as this one.

As stated before, this book is not final in the field that it covers; at best it is only a stepping-stone to the higher realm of spiritual consciousness, toward attainment of the mind "which was also in Christ Jesus."

Selections From the
Metaphysical Bible Dictionary[1]

Aaron, aâr'-ŏn (Heb.)—*illumined*; *enlightener*; *mountaineer* (very lofty).

Brother of Moses; of the Israelitish tribe of Levi, and first high priest of Israel (Exod. 6:20, 28:1–4).

Meta. Executive power of divine law. Aaron, the first high priest of Israel and the bearer of intellectual light to the Israelites, signifies the ruling power of the intellectual consciousness. The making of the "molten calf" by Aaron (Exod. 32:1–8) signifies the false states of thought (idols) that man builds into his consciousness when he perceives the Truth but does not carry his spiritual ideals into execution, choosing instead to let his thoughts function in a lower plane of consciousness.

In Exodus 40:12, 13, Aaron and his sons typify spiritual strength, which becomes the presiding, directive power of a new state of consciousness. Through spiritual strength there is set up an abiding thought action that contributes to the building of the holy Temple (redeemed body). Bringing Aaron and his sons to the door of the tent of meeting and washing them with water means that we should declare spiritual strength to be the presiding, directive power of this new state of consciousness—not a mere animal strength, but a strength purified from all grossness of sense. This declaration of strength is absolutely necessary to the permanency of the body tabernacle. Through it is set up an abiding thought action that continues while one's attention is elsewhere: Aaron continues to minister in his priestly office.

Abaddon, ă-băd'-dōn (Heb.)—de-*stroyer*; *destruction*.

Called Apollyon, in the Greek tongue. Said to be king over the great army of locusts that came out from the abyss to destroy (Rev. 9:2–11).

*Meta.*That this name has reference to a very destructive belief of man's is evident from the meaning of the name and from the 9th chapter of Revelation. From Exodus 10:14, 15, and Joel 2:3–10 (compare these texts with their references and you will see that they all are speaking of the same thing), one can get an idea of the destructiveness of the locusts of Palestine and the surrounding countries. They quite commonly came up like great armies and ate every living plant in their path; also, the leaves and the branches of the trees. So Abaddon must stand for the error belief in utter destruction of life and form.

The true life principle can never be destroyed; only the outer form of man's belief in materiality is destructible. So long as man believes in materiality or destruction, the outer destruction of forms will take place. It is very necessary, therefore, that the thought of the possibility of life's being destructible, or in any way limited, be erased entirely from the consciousness. "There is only one Presence and one Power in the universe—the Good omnipotent." Life is omnipresent, eternal, sure; life cannot be destroyed, because it is God Himself.

Abagtha, ă-băg'-thá (Pers.)—*happy, prosperous.*

One of the seven eunuchs, or chamberlains, who served in the palace of Ahasuerus, King of Persia (Esther 1:10).

Meta. A eunuch, in consciousness, represents a thought from which the capacity to increase life and its forms has been eliminated. The chamberlain, in this instance, is a keeper of the king's bed-chamber. . . .

Baal, bā'-ăl (Heb.)—*lord; master; possessor; owner; guardian; a husband; Jove; Jupiter; the sun* . . . a generic term for God in many of the Syro-Arabian languages.

Chief male deity of the Phoenicians and Canaanites, as Ashtoreth was their principal female deity (Judg. 2:13). The worship of Baal was directed to Jovis, Jupiter, or the Sun as the guardian and giver of good fortune, prosperity, and abundance.

Meta. Baal means *Lord*, and it was the besetting sin of the ancient Hebrews to apply this title to things formed instead of the formless. This tendency is still prevalent, and not merely among the Hebrews.

All concepts of God as less than universal mind are Baal. Those who believe in a personal god are Baal worshipers, because they make an image of that which is "without body, parts, or passions." They should learn to go back of the realm of things, that they may come in touch with God, who is Spirit, mind, cause, omnipresence.

Baal worship was a form of nature worship. All people who study materiality and seek to find in it the source of existence are sacrificing to Baal. This is strictly intellectual. But there are those on the soul plane who think that they are spiritual because they feel the throb of nature and join in all her moods. They are closely allied to the whirling dervish, and dissipate their soul substance in the various forces of nature with which they are in love. Such persons must do away with this Baal worship and call upon the life-fire of the Spirit to consume every material phase of sacrifice.

Baalim and Asheroth represent nature in its various sensuous aspects. . . .

Baalah, bā'-ăl-ăh (Heb.)—*lady; mistress; possessor; guardian; sorceress; citizenship; a citizen.*

A border town of Judah. Kiriath-jearim is another name for this city (Josh. 15:9).

Meta. An innate consciousness of authority and ownership in man, a consciousness that pertains to the feminine or affectional nature, the soul (mistress, possessor), and is expressed in the psychic and material to the point of idolatry. (See **Baal**.)

Baalath, bā'-ăl-ăth (Heb.)—*citizens; subjects; possessions; belonging to Baal; mistresses.*

a. A town of the tribe of Dan (Josh. 19:44).

b. A town that Solomon rebuilt after he married the daughter of the king of Egypt (1 Kings 9:18). This latter was perhaps the same place as the previously named town of the tribe of Dan.

Meta. Baal means *lord, master, possessor*, and pertains to the attributing of power and authority to the outer world of phenomena instead of recognizing Spirit as the one true source of all existence and of all prosperity and supply. Baalath represents the belief of the spiritually unawakened soul in man that his possessions, his privileges, and the good that he enjoys have their source in the outer, the material.

Baalath-beer, bā'-ăl-ăth-bēr (Heb.)—*city of the well; place of the well; lady of the well; mistress of the well; subjects of the pit.*

A city of Canaan that was allotted to the Israelitish tribe of Simeon (Josh. 19:8); Baal of 1 Chronicles 4:33 may be the same city.

Meta. Baal-beer, *meaning city of the well, place of the well, . . .*

Ruth (Heb.)—*female friend; sympathetic compassion; desirable; delightful; friendship; pleasing; beautiful.*

A Moabitess who became the wife of Boaz, an Israelitish man of Bethlehem-Judah. David was descended from her. Ruth was the daughter-in-law of Naomi and returned with her from Moab to Bethlehem-Judah (Ruth 1 to 4).

Meta. The love of the soul in its natural state, or the love of the natural soul for God and for the things of Spirit.

Ruth is a type of the beautiful, the pure, and the loving characteristics of the natural man (*sympathetic companion, friendship, female friend, delightful, desirable, beautiful*). She was the one and only good that Naomi took with her back to Bethlehem-Judah (divine substance, the real).

In Ruth's words in Ruth 1:16 is represented human love raised to divine love by its willingness to leave the love of the unreal, to follow after the real, to go wherever true love leads, to be steadfast in that love; in other words, to love in the highest and best degree and to acknowledge and worship always the God of love.

Ruth's loyalty to God and the spiritual life was rewarded, just as such loyalty always is. Boaz and Ruth were ancestors of King David and of David's greater son, Jesus the Christ. Here we have the progression of a thought from simple, loving obedience and devotion to a mighty ruler of worlds. Thus spiritual thought grows—very quietly and slowly at first, but gradually increasing—until it finally carries all before it.

sabachthani, sā-băch-thā'-nī (Grk. Fr. Chald.)—*thou hast forsaken me; thou hast Left me (to what) hast thou surrendered me? (why) hast thou forsaken me?*

In *sabachthani* we find the root idea of loosening, setting free; letting alone and forsaking are secondary developments. The real root idea of the word expresses the cutting loose of bondage, or freeing from slavery.

On the cross Jesus cried, "Eli, Eli, lama sabachthani? That is, My God, my God, why hast thou forsaken me?" (Matt. 27:46).

Meta. The cry of the soul at the darkest hour of crucifixion. When the sensual is passing away it seems as though man were giving up all his life, including every good. The sensual looms so large at this hour that for the time being it shuts God from the consciousness of the individual who is going through the experience. But God never forsakes His children; there can be no real separation from the Divine, and a glorious resurrection into a greater degree of spiritual life than was ever realized before always follows each letting go of the old. "Even so reckon ye also yourselves to be dead unto sin, but alive unto God in Christ Jesus." "That like as Christ was raised from the dead through the glory of the Father, so we also might walk in newness of life."

Sabaoth, să-bā'-ōth (Gk. fr. Heb.)—armies; hosts.

The Greek form of the Hebrew word for armies or hosts; generally used with Jehovah as Jehovah of hosts, and meaning Jehovah as ruler over the whole earth and heaven (Rom. 9:29).

Meta. The significance of "Lord of Sabaoth," or "Jehovah of hosts," in individual consciousness is that the Jehovah, Christ, true I AM in one, is Lord of—has dominion over—all the host of thoughts, forces, and activities in one's whole organism, in mind (heaven) and body (earth). . . .

Woman, Greek of Mark 7:25–30; also the woman with the alabaster cruise of ointment (Matt. 26:7).

Meta. Besides the interpretation given under **SYROPHOENICIAN** (which see), the Greek woman of Tyre and Sidon may also be said to represent the unspiritualized love that is natural to the body. Her daughter is physical sensation, which has been sensualized by impure thought.

Whenever the illumined I AM (Jesus) centers its attention anywhere in the body, there is at once a quickening of intelligence and a reaching out for higher things by the consciousness functioning there. Every part of the organism is under the control of a set of thoughts that direct and care for that particular function. The nerves are under the control of a thought that thinks about nerves; the muscles, bones, blood—every department of the man has its distinct thought center. So we are made up of many men and many women, because the masculine and feminine qualities are equally distributed and they all work together in harmony when divine order is established.

We use all these different parts of our being, but not understandingly. In our ignorance we dissipate the natural purity and strength of these obedient people who form our soul and our body; but when we become illumined by Spirit a reform sets in, and they all reflect the new light that has come to us, especially so when we concentrate our mind on the life centers, or "enter into a house" (Mark 7:24).

There lingers in the mind that old idea, borrowed from the limited vision of the Jew, that Spirit does not include the body in its redemptive process, but the body cries out for cleansing and purification. "Even the dogs under the table eat of the children's crumbs." Good common sense should teach us that life is always present throughout nature, a stream proceeding from the highest to the lowest.

The woman with the "alabaster cruse of exceeding precious ointment" (Matt. 26:7) signifies the forgiving love of Spirit, and her ointment is the conserved nerve fluid that is stored up in the secret recesses of the body.

The disciples thought that this precious ointment should be sold and the proceeds given to the poor, because they were in the outer consciousness where there is a seeming lack of vitality at times, and, not understanding the law of conservation, they thought that their "poor" needs should be supplied first.

Jesus was passing through the regeneration, and the sense consciousness of the flesh body was being crucified. The precious substance of love was consumed to the end that it might be brought forth as the vitalizing element of His resurrected body. This is what Jesus meant when He said that the ointment that the woman poured upon His body was preparation for His burial. . . .

Word, of God.

Meta. John gives us the following concerning the Word of God: "In the beginning was the Word, and the Word was with God, and the Word was God." The Word of God is the divine Logos, God in His capacity as creative power, and includes all the potentialities of Being. It is the idea of God, the image and likeness of God, spiritual man. In it are all the possibilities, all the qualities, of God.

Being, the original fount, is an impersonal principle; but in its work of creation it puts forth an idea that contains all ideas: the Logos, Word,

Christ, the Son of God, or spiritual man. This spiritual man or Christ, the Word of God, is the true inner self of every individual. . . .

. . . through their being received by the mind and carried into the body through the subconsciousness by one's thought. Constructive words that renew the body are made a part of the body consciousness by prayer and meditation. . . .

Wrath, of God.

Meta. Some Bible authorities claim that the "wrath of God," or of the Lord (Rom. 1:18), might with equal propriety be translated the "blessings" of the Lord. We know that after the destruction of limited and inferior thoughts and forms of life, other and higher thoughts and forms take their place, and the change is actually a blessing in the end. So even the "wrath" that comes to our fleshly tabernacles, when we persist in holding them in material thought, is a blessing ultimately. When we are loving and nonresistant we do not suffer under the transformations that go on when the Mosaic law is being carried out.

The "wrath of God' is really the working out of the law of Being destructively or inharmoniously for the individual who does not conform to the law but thinks and acts in opposition to it.

Charles Fillmore in His Own Words: A Radio Interview Given in 1936, and a Radio Talk (Undated)

Radio Interview

Question: Mr. Fillmore, you are one of the founders and still active offi-
cials of the Unity School of Christianity of Kansas City, Missouri?[1]
Answer: Yes.

Q: When was the Unity School begun?
A: Unity began about fifty years ago, as it was, then we started having
study classes, but we usually reckon the real beginning as April 1889 as
that was when we issued our first monthly periodical, the *Unity Magazine*.

Q: Mr. Fillmore, what is your age?
A: In about two months, I will have completed my 82nd year.

Q: And, Mr. Fillmore, you are still actively engaged in carrying on the
work of the Unity School?
A: Yes. I deliver six lectures regularly every week and some extras. Write
several articles monthly for the *Unity Magazine*. Have written two books
in the past twelve months besides taking two extensive lecture tours, one
in Colorado, and the other in the eastern states down to Florida. Have
no idea of retiring but shall continue the Unity work with renewed interest and enthusiasm always.

Q: Mr. Fillmore, to what do you attribute your good health and your ability to continue your rather strenuous work beyond the age where most
men experience mental and physical decline, if not death?
A: When I began the study of the doctrine of Jesus Christ I was a bodily
wreck. At the age of ten, I had been afflicted with tuberculosis of the

hip—was very lame and suffered continually. The doctors said the abscesses on my leg would kill me before I was forty. I was not a Christian, but when I began to study what Jesus taught in the Bible about God as the source of life and health, I had faith that I could be healed. From that time, I began to improve in health. I have improved gradually and now teach and believe that man can demonstrate what Jesus taught: "If any one keeps my word, he will never see death" [John 8:51].

Q: Mr. Fillmore, do you believe that the healing power of God, as taught by Jesus and demonstrated so strikingly by you, can be applied by all persons?

A: I can conceive no possible reason why the healing system of Jesus cannot be applied by all persons who will accept it. Jesus demonstrated it by healing great multitudes and He commissioned His disciples to go forth and preach the gospel, cast out demons, and heal the sick. The New Testament proved that the Holy Spirit bore witness to their divine commission by the signs that followed, in other words, they cast out demons and healed the sick by using the healing system taught them by Jesus. We are teaching that body healing is fundamental in Christianity and thousands are being healed every year. Our healing demonstrations have been going on for fifty years.

Q: Mr. Fillmore, could you, in a few words, tell us what the fundamental principles are in the healing system taught by Jesus?

A: To understand and become efficient in the use of the healing system taught and used by Jesus requires study and experience. Sometimes the underlying principle of faith in God as the omnipresent Spirit of life and health is quickly grasped by the student, but this must be followed up by a further realization of the cooperation of the Holy Spirit as the helper of those who have faith in God as the health of His people.

Q: Mr. Fillmore, do you understand and teach that physical healing is the main objective of the doctrine of Jesus?

A: By no means. Physical healing is merely the partial product of the soul salvation accomplished by following the guidance of the Lord Jesus Christ.

Q: Jesus claimed that in no other way could we escape the race ills of mind, body, and affairs except by following Him. Do you believe that, and does your experience in handling race thoughts convince you that Jesus knew what He was talking about?

A: I am satisfied that Jesus was a master of mind forces and that He broke the spell of evil or satanic thoughts that has for ages bound humanity. All those who look to Jesus for help will be mentally freed from the race insanity of sin, sickness, greed, hate, poverty, and death. Also, they will all be eventually gathered together here on earth and form the nucleus of a new and higher civilization for this planet. The disintegration of the old civilization is close at hand, and those who have been following Jesus in the spiritual life are preparing to get together and establish His kingdom here on earth.

Q: Mr. Fillmore, what is the object of Unity?

A: The object of Unity, concisely stated, is to educate people in the fundamental principles of Christianity and quicken and make active in everyone the innate spiritual life of man.

Q: Mr. Fillmore, do you think that the popular Christian world does not understand the fundamental principles of Christianity?

A: The popular Christian world does not understand the scientific principles upon which Christianity is founded. The popular Christian religion teaches faith as the foundation of Christianity, but in addition to faith, which we stress emphatically, we add understanding of the mind and how it operates to build soul and body.

Q: Do I understand, Mr. Fillmore, that you make psychology a part of your study of Christian principles?

A: Certainly. Psychology pertains to the soul, and soul salvation is an important part of the teaching of Jesus.

Q: Mr. Fillmore, I understand there are hundreds of "Unity Centers" in various parts of the world where the doctrines of Unity are taught and the literature distributed. Is Unity a church?

A: No. Unity is not a church and we strive to keep its centers undenominational. However, as the students of the centers organize, they tend to form what appears to be church groups, but the majority of our students are regular members of orthodox churches.

A Radio Talk (Undated)

Ideas, we are told, rule the world. Accepting this old axiom as true, it logically follows that man should exercise wisdom in the selection of his ideas, also the source from which he draws them. Emerson says that when a man appears with revolutionary ideas, kings totter on their thrones. In our day, there are few kings left to totter—there have been too many men with revolutionary ideas.

As we inquire into the character of those with revolutionary minds, we find that they derive their ideas from an apparently original source, and we seek to know what it is and what relation it bears to the minds of the common herd. In nearly every instance, these great reformers claim that they are moved by a higher power. They give various names to the source of their inspirations but, invariably, they protest against the old order of things, whether it be politics, religion, or what not.

Jesus, the greatest of all religious reformers, said that His inspiration was the Father and that it inspired Him from within. He said that the words He spoke were not His, but the Father dwelling within him. It has been assumed that Jesus was the only begotten of God and that He had abilities superior to all other men. However, an unbiased study of His teaching reveals that He did not claim any privileged ability because of His sonship, but that all who arrive at the same degree of spiritual development that He had would have equal and even greater abilities. He said, "He who believes in me will also do the works that I do; and greater works than these will he do" [John 14:12].

Undoubtedly, the greatest discovery, the most important revelation to the inhabitants of this planet was that there was a mind which man could contact within himself, and by and through that contact open the way for the abilities of a genius. Modern psychology confirms what Jesus taught about the unlimited capacity of the Super Mind in man.

The Super Mind has always sporadically manifested its super ability, and those who made the contact have shone out as the rare geniuses of the race. But Jesus is the only great genius who plainly taught that what He possessed in super ability was possible of possession by all men.

Discipline of certain faculties of the mind was stressed by Jesus; among them, faith was given first place. Raising faith out of its usual material field of action and giving it the freedom of unlimited spiritual ideas, Jesus said, would make man master of his material limitations. He taught that we could even remove mountains through faith.

Our modern philosophers tell us that we are using but a small part of the innate capacity of our mind or body. Our muscles can, by training, be strengthened until we stand forth as physical giants. Our lungs can be expanded to unbelievable capacity. So (it can be) with every function of our body. It is full of stored-up, unused elements of various kinds waiting our mental release. It is through the mind that we move upon the cells of the body, and it is in the higher or upper ranges of the mind that we shall find the power to release the pent-up energies of the body.

Jesus developed the Super Mind, which he called the Father, and thereby performed what men have called miracles. But there are no miracles, if we mean by that word acts that bring about events without the intervention of law. What seems a miracle is a performance under a law with which we are not yet acquainted.

Jesus developed faith spiritually until the atomic energy of His body became obedient to His will and He could walk upon the water. His accomplishments were so far in advance of the ordinary man that He was declared a God, and regarded as having a divine birth and heavenly prerogatives, none of which He assumed. When He walked upon the water, He reproved Peter, who failed in his attempt to do likewise. He said to him, "Oh, man of little faith, why do you doubt?" [Matt 14:31]. So it is found that faith is one of the mind factors that have to do with the release of the hidden forces of the soul and body of man.

Jesus tried to teach His followers how they might do what He did. He did not claim to be superior to other men in His *so-called* divine power. He said, "He who believes in me will also do the works that I do; and greater works than these will he do" [John 14:12]. Men have not dared to attempt to do the things that Jesus did because those in religious authority have claimed that they were evidences of His divinity, and that it is sacrilegious for mere man even to attempt to do what Jesus did. Thus, man retarded the development of his mind and has belittled himself as a poor worm of the dust and exalted Jesus as a god until a great gulf has been formed across which none have dared to venture. But our modern men of science are telling us that our bodies are heavily charged with dynamic energies that, if released, would make us the most powerful beings in the world.

For instance, a recent report of a conclave of scientists says that they talked about the marvelous possibilities in the release of electronic energy locked up in atoms; that in one pound of water there is ten million horsepower. The Earl of Birkenhead once said, "Give man that atomic energy and he can alter the climate and geography of the world." Yet, man's body is ninety percent water, and with every thought and act he is releasing some of its energy. Who shall say that this release of energy shall be limited to ordinary muscular or brain action?

Through the impact of a more dynamic mind, it is within reason to assume that man might increase his brain capacity a thousand-fold. Jesus said to His followers, "If you have faith as a grain of mustard seed (atom), you will say to this mountain, 'Move hence to yonder place' and it will move; and nothing will be impossible to you" [Matt. 17:20].

Here we have the declaration of a Master Mind that nothing shall be impossible to man if he develops that subtle and little understood attribute of the mind named faith.

Faith has been associated with a species of blind fanatical belief in the supernatural until logical minds that seek an understanding of the principles underlying their religious conviction have classed its exponents as subjects of a sort of ecclesiastical delusion. That faith might be a faculty with dynamic power equal to the release of hidden forces in the natural world has not occurred to scientifically trained minds.

However, a new type of scientific mind is being trained in this age of phenomenal discoveries. This mind is not content with the materialism of the evolutionary schools of science, nor the spirituality of the religious schools. The evolutionist and the modernist are both respected and their views accepted up to a certain point, but not considered as the final revelation of either science or religion.

Schools of scientific mental discipline are being established in which the mind is subject to fearless research as to its ability to react to certain ideas both religious and secular. The Unity School of Christianity is of this character. It is inquiring into all thought processes—how thought acts upon man in the mechanical, emotional, and reasoning zones of his being. Some unusual results have been obtained from this unbiased research into the mental sources of the dominant traits of the human race. Not the least of these has been the discovery that the mind of man has possibilities far beyond anything achieved in the past or imagined for the future.

This study of the mind in its higher aspects of faith and love reveals that it has three primal fields of action: the spiritual, the intellectual, and the physical. Also, that these three zones are as well defined in the mental world as are the zones of radioactivity in the physical. The man who thinks physically is mentally chained to his physical plane, and the man who thinks intellectually cannot rise above his plane of logic and comparison. Only the man who thinks spiritually, who trains his mind to handle ideas unhindered by dimension, comparison, or human limitations, attains the supremacy of a Master Mind. History records only one such mind, that of Jesus Christ.

It is not claimed that this Unity has produced an equal of Jesus Christ, nor that it ever will produce His equal, but it is claimed that what He did, and what He said we could do if we followed Him, has been demonstrated in part, and enough proven to insure the fulfillment of all His promises to those who adopt and apply His methods.

It is impossible to give in a short lesson such as this more than a hint of the tremendous powers locked up in the mind and body of man. It is enough to say that our bodies have stored within them all the energies that we have touched in thought and act during the millions of years that we have existed on this planet. Jesus said that His body was the temple of the living God. Jesus, according to the Scriptures, took on the body of the race and what was true of His body is true of the bodies of us all.

You ask, how shall we release and get the benefit of these pent-up experiences of man stored in his subconsciousness since the beginning? Jesus taught in parables, figures, and stories how to do this very thing. By studying His methods of concentrating the mind on the super realm of ideas and then projecting these ideas into the body, we attain at first a theoretical understanding of the law. Then, this understanding must be applied by doing the work of releasing the imprisoned ideas, both good and bad, as He released them, when, for example, He loosed the demons imprisoned in the tombs and drove them into the swine. This so-called miracle is a symbolic illustration of how to eliminate from the body certain imprisoned discordant energies. These are the erratic thoughts that the ego inhibited in some previous incarnation which, if left in the imprisoned cells, will eventually break loose and destroy the body. It is these violent thought entities which we have generated in our mind that finally destroy our body. Under the instruction of the Master Mind, Jesus, we are told in symbols how to cast out these errors and save ourselves from sickness and body deterioration.

This is but a single illustration of the numerous lessons that are taught to us by the great physician, Jesus Christ. He opened up to the whole human family a new kingdom which He called the "kingdom of the heavens." He did not name this higher kingdom as a place but as a higher attainment by man of his innate possibilities. He said, "The kingdom of God is in the midst of you" [Luke 17:21]. We are on the verge of tremendously important discoveries about man and his relation to the universe. Nearly all of our scientific discoveries so far have been located in the environment of man. Now we are seeking to know more about the dominant inhabitant of that environment, which is man.

The great English scientist, Sir James Jeans, says that science is finding that God is a great mathematician. Those who study the esoteric side of Jesus' teaching find that there is a science in which thoughts and words are scientifically related in rate of vibration or power, compression or love, wavelength or poise, etc.

All things can be resolved into the primal ideas from which they originally sprang and by which they are sustained. This great truth is epitomized in the first chapter of John's gospel where it is written, "In the beginning was the Word, and the Word was with God, and the Word was God. He was in the beginning with God; all things were made through him and without him was not anything made that was made. In him was life, and the life was the light of men" [John 1:1–4]. In this is restated, in epitomized form, the "God said" of the first chapter of Genesis.

This formative power of thought and word has been passed on by Creative Mind to man, his "image and likeness," and experimentation with thoughts and words proves that there is a definite movement in cell life, especially in the human organism, when certain kinds of words are focused upon them. Thus is being worked out a mathematical relation between the thoughts and words of man and their effects in his body, proving the truth of Jesus' statement that, "By your words you will be justified, and by your words you will be condemned" [Matt. 12:37].

Note: In his Unity book, *The Twelve Powers of Man*, Charles Fillmore expressed his thought about the power of the *spoken word* when amplified through radio broadcasts. He said, "If the spoken word can be mechanically intensified a hundred million times, how much greater will be its power when energized by Spirit!"

Early New Thought Movement Participants

1688–1772   Emanuel Swedenborg
Teacher, author, spiritual philosopher, and prominent scientist in Swe-
den. He developed a theological system of beliefs, adopted by those who
refer to themselves as "Swedenborgians." His first theological writings
were published in 1748; his visions and writings inspired his followers to
establish the Church of the New Jerusalem, often shortened to the "New
Church." New Thought historian J. Gordon Melton states that Swedenborg's influence on New Thought is inestimable as exemplified in the
Bible interpretations in Charles Fillmore's *Metaphysical Bible Dictionary*
and in Mary Baker Eddy's *Science and Health with Key to the Scriptures*.

1735–1815   Franz Mesmer
Viennese psychiatrist who developed theory of "animal magnetism," a
belief that thoughts could be transferable. He used hypnosis, suggestion,
and laying-on of hands in his practice. He was a major influence in the development of New Thought and also of Mary Baker Eddy in her early years.

Not available   Charles Poyen
Brought Mesmerism to America and Phineas Parkhurst Quimby heard
him in 1838.

1802–1866   Phineas Parkhurst Quimby
Dedicated his adult life to healing and the study of it. He was a key influ-
encer in the development of New Thought. Some label him as the founder of the movement; however, this is an overstatement. Many of those
instrumental in the development of New Thought such as Mary Baker
Eddy and Julius and Annetta Dresser studied the work of Quimby,
although they learned of him from the work and writings of Warren Felt
Evans because Quimby's writings were locked in Washington and
unavailable to them.

1803–1882   **Ralph Waldo Emerson**

American essayist and poet, a leader of the philosophical movement of transcendentalism, which every stream of New Thought incorporates. He was ordained a Unitarian minister, as was his father, and gave the address at Harvard Divinity School in 1839. His father served the First Unitarian Church and Ralph served the Second Unitarian Church, both in Boston. In a history of New Thought, Emmet Fox wrote that Emerson was the founder of the movement. This is not true, although his thoughts did influence the early stages of New Thought development.

1817–1889   **Warren Felt Evans**

New Thought author and healer. He was among the first to write of healing as taught and practiced by Phineas Parkhurst Quimby. Evans was a Swedenborgian and he integrated the philosophies of Emanuel Swedenborg and Quimby and, to some degree, Franz Anton Mesmer. Several New Thought historians believe that the literary efforts of Evans in synthesizing the work of Swedenborg and Quimby is more important to the New Thought movement than the work of Quimby himself.

1821–1910   **Mary Baker Eddy**

Founded Church of Christ, Scientist, 1881. She was initially a student in the growing New Thought movement, but she became insular and separated herself and her organization from the movement and its outgrowths, such as Religious Science, Divine Science, and Unity.

1838–1893   **Julius Dresser and**
Not Available   **Annetta (Seabury) Dresser**

They met Phineas Parkhurst Quimby in 1860, and because they supported and practiced his work, they were among the first to effectively organize what has since been called New Thought. In fact, the couple was so effective in organization of New Thought that they have even been named by some as the founders of New Thought, but they were not. They were serious students who worked to advance the cause of New Thought.

1842–1910   **William James**

A famous American psychologist and philosopher who was also an avid student of Phineas Parkhurst Quimby. James's lectures and his written work, such as *Varieties of Religious Experience,* were intellectual in the extreme even as he discussed how humankind "feels" nature and holds religious beliefs. He even included himself in these observations of humankind. It may have been Quimby's dislike for organized religion that influenced James's circumspect approach to religion, despite James's acknowledgment that most people in most cultures have a need for a "God" and seem to have an intimate relationship with their deity.

1844–1906   Malinda E. Cramer

Student of Emma Curtis Hopkins and established the first New Thought movement, which she named Divine Science. In 1888, she established the Home College of Divine Science in San Francisco. She began traveling to teach and eventually became aware of Nona Brooks, who also called her work Divine Science. Brooks studied briefly with Cramer who encouraged Brooks to continue to call her work Divine Science.

1845–1921   Ursula Gestefeld

Founded Science of Being and the Church of New Thought after writing a book about Christian Science that displeased Mary Baker Eddy to the point that she denounced Gestefeld publicly.

1845–1931   Myrtle Fillmore

Cofounded the Unity School of Christianity with her husband, Charles S. Fillmore, in April 1889, which was marked by their first magazine publication *Modern Thought*, which was later renamed *Unity* in 1895. She studied the teachings of Emma Curtis Hopkins, who ordained her in 1891. Later, in 1906, she was one of the first people to be ordained as a Unity minister. Aside from founding and developing Unity with her husband, Myrtle founded *Wee Wisdom*, the first children's magazine in the United States, in August 1893.

1847–1918   Thomas Troward

A judge, he was also a key figure in mental science instruction, of which he taught and wrote about. His involvement in mental science instruction made him an influential figure in the development of Ernest Holmes's Science of Mind, and Troward's writings also influenced the Religious Science movement, which Holmes founded.

1848–1908   Althea B. Small

Student of Emma Curtis Hopkins. With the help of others and her sisters Nona Brooks and Fannie James, she helped influence the Divine Science movement in Denver. In 1898, she and her sisters, with the help of others, established the Denver Church and College of Divine Science.

1848–1941   Emilie Cady

Homeopathic physician and author, she was a student of Hopkins and a good friend of the Fillmores, although she never visited Kansas City. She wrote two classic volumes, *Lessons in Truth* (originally published as a series in *Modern Thought*) and *How I Used Truth*, which are still used as basic textbooks by Unity and New Thought students.

1854–1917   Charles Brodie Patterson

President of the International Metaphysical League and then became the first president of the New Thought Federation. He was editor and author of several New Thought publications in addition to being widely read in New Thought.

1854–1914   Fannie B. James

Student of Mabel McCoy, a classmate of Mrs. Frank (Kate) Bingham. Along with her sisters, Nona Brooks and Althea B. Small, she helped organize the Divine Science movement in Denver.

1854–1948   Charles Fillmore

Cofounded the Unity School of Christianity with his wife, Myrtle, in 1889. Emma Curtis Hopkins ordained him in 1891, as well as his wife, and he was later ordained as one of the first Unity ministers in 1906. Charles was an instrumental leader of Unity until his death, and wrote the *Metaphysical Bible Dictionary*, among other books.

1853–1925   Emma Curtis Hopkins

Is known as the "teacher of teachers" as she taught and influenced many key people in the New Thought movement, including Charles and Myrtle Fillmore, Ernest Holmes, Malinda Cramer, and Mrs. Frank (Kate) Bingham. Hopkins was to the New Thought movement what the Apostle Paul was to Christianity. Had it been left to the twelve disciples,

Christianity may only be a word of antiquity by now. Since Mary Baker Eddy excommunicated so many of her students (Hopkins was one of them) and so many left willingly, New Thought may have died completely if it had not been for Hopkins.

Not Available **Mrs. Frank (Kate) Bingham**
A student of Emma Curtis Hopkins and graduated from the Emma Curtis Hopkins College of Christian Science in Chicago in 1886. She introduced metaphysical healing to Nona Brooks.

Not Available **Harriet Rix**
Cofounder of the Homes of Truth in 1888.

1858–1924 **Annie (Rix) Militz and**
Not Available **Paul Militz**
Both studied with Emma Curtis Hopkins and graduated from her school. The couple married in the 1890s. Annie cofounded the Homes of Truth with Harriet Rix in 1888, and was also editor and publisher of *Master Mind*, an early New Thought magazine.

1861–1945 **Nona Brooks**
Student of Mrs. Frank (Kate) Bingham, who studied with Hopkins. Brooks called what she taught Divine Science with her sisters Althea B. Small and Fannie B. James. The sisters later met Malinda E. Cramer, who founded a separate Divine Science in California in 1888. With the encouragement of Cramer, Brooks and her sisters created the First Church and College of Divine Science in Denver, Colorado, in 1898.

1861–1947 **Alfred North Whitehead**
A mathematician and New Thought philosopher and author. He published many books on mathematics, natural sciences, metaphysics, theory of knowledge, education, religion, and history. He was interested in the relationship of science and religion.

1864–1941 **Albert C. Grier**
Ordained as a minister in the Universalist Church in Spokane, Washington. Grier became a prominent leader in New Thought movement. He

worked closely with Ernest Holmes and leaders in both Eastern and Western traditions of religion.

1866–1958   Ralph Waldo Trine

A philosopher, mystic, teacher, prolific author, and early mentor of the New Thought movement. He became known as a self-help author long before it became a popular genre of literature.

1874–1948   Christian D. Larson

An early author of numerous self-help books and a prominent leader in New Thought. He greatly influenced Ernest Holmes, who studied with Larson.

1882–1964   Joel Goldsmith

A monumental teacher of practical mysticism and founder of The Infinite Way. He was a prolific author, and his most well-known book is *The Art of Meditation*.

1883–1973   Fenwicke L. Holmes

The older brother of Ernest Holmes. Together they created the Metaphysical Institute in 1918 and taught what they called Mental Science, named after the magazine they began. After organizing this institute, Fenwicke stayed east and his brother moved west and eventually established the Institute of Religious Science and Philosophy.

1886–1961   Emmet Fox

Asked Charles Fillmore to ordain him as a Unity minister, which Charles would not do without Fox taking classes. He was later ordained in the Divine Science branch of New Thought and was a prominent New Thought author. He was also a major supporter of Charles and Myrtle Fillmore and wrote several tracts published by Unity School. Fox was also instrumental in establishing Alcoholics Anonymous, and his book, *Sermon on the Mount*, was used as its first "Big Book" in early years.

1887–1967   Walter C. Lanyon

Ordained by Emma Curtis Hopkins. He was a prolific New Thought Christian writer, having authored more than forty books.

1887–1960   **Ernest Holmes**

Ernest first studied New Thought in Boston, and he and his brother, Fenwicke, worked together in the east and created the Metaphysical Institute in 1918. Later, the brothers taught, published a magazine, and each wrote a book about their movement, Mental Science. Later, Ernest moved to California and in 1927 was ordained by Agnes Galler of Divine Science-Seattle. The year before, Ernest wrote *The Science of Mind* and, with his magazine of the same name, founded the organization Institute of Religious Science and Philosophy, which eventually broke into two groups. One was a church-like format and in 1953 became the United Church of Religious Science. The second group became Religious Science International. Ernest was widely read and was influenced by Emerson, Troward, and Hopkins, whom he studied with shortly before her death.

1893–1985   **Masaharu Taniguchi**

Founded Seicho-No-Ie, the Truth of Life movement, in Japan in 1930. He spoke at a Unity ministers' conference at Unity Village in the 1960s, at the invitation of Sig Paulson, former director of World Outreach at Unity School of Christianity, during one of Taniguchi's U.S. lecture tours. Seicho-No-Ie is a religion that originated in Japan. However, Taniguchi acknowledged that while he was reading, comparing, and contrasting with his own thinking on the subject of religion, he was exposed to Christian Science through Ernest Holmes's Mental Science.

1904–1971   **Mildred Mahn**

Metaphysical teacher and author. She founded the Society of Pragmatic Mysticism.

1921–   **Charles R. Fillmore**

Grandson of cofounders of the Unity School of Christianity. In 1965, as executive vice president of Unity School of Christianity, he requested that Unity field ministers create a sister organization to facilitate all activities having to do with service to and self-governance of Unity ministries, which they did. They named it the Association of Unity Churches (now the Association of Unity Churches, International).

1936–   **Angelo Pizelo**
Founder and director of the Emerson Theological Institute, established
1992. The Institute is a New Thought School of Ministry and the primary
education arm of the Affiliated New Thought Network.

Not Available   **Johnnie Colemon**
Originally ordained a Unity minister, she had a new vision and founded
the Universal Foundation for Better Living and the Johnnie Colemon
School of Ministry, Chicago, Illinois, in 1974.

Not Available   **Barbara King**
A minister and author, Barbara founded the Hillside Chapel and Truth
Center International and the Barbara King School of Ministry in Atlanta,
Georgia, in 1971.

1940–   **Matthew Fox**
A former Catholic priest, and now an Episcopal priest, in 1996 he
founded University of Creation Spirituality (renamed Wisdom University in 2005). He has just announced a program that will ordain ministers, and his new spiritual community is not yet named but will be a
"Creation-Centered Church/Spiritual Community" as outlined in his e-
newsletter of November 25, 2005.

1956–   **Harry Morgan Moses**
Was ordained by Religious Science International (RSI). After a disagree-
ment with the RSI administration, his ordination was rescinded in early
1992. He and colleague-friend Dominic Polifrone, whose ordination
also was rescinded in 1991, collaborated to found Affiliated New
Thought Network (ANTN). Initially it was created to support Religious
Science ministers who considered they were independent from Reli-
gious Science International, and then opened itself to serve any Religious
Science ministers. Over time, ANTN began providing support for all
New Thought ministers who were independent.

1939–   **Dominic Polifrone**

After rescission of his Religious Science International (RSI) ordination over a disagreement with RSI administration in 1991, he co-created the Affiliated New Thought Network (ANTN) with his friend and colleague, Harry Morgan Moses, in 1992. ANTN was originally created as a support system for independent Religious Science ministers, and over time was opened to all independent New Thought ministers.

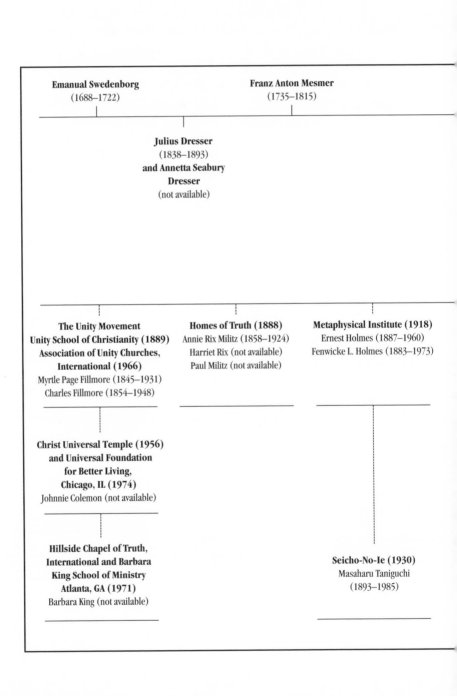

Emanual Swedenborg
(1688–1722)

Franz Anton Mesmer
(1735–1815)

Julius Dresser
(1838–1893)
and Annetta Seabury
Dresser
(not available)

The Unity Movement
Unity School of Christianity (1889)
Association of Unity Churches,
International (1966)
Myrtle Page Fillmore (1845–1931)
Charles Fillmore (1854–1948)

Homes of Truth (1888)
Annie Rix Militz (1858–1924)
Harriet Rix (not available)
Paul Militz (not available)

Metaphysical Institute (1918)
Ernest Holmes (1887–1960)
Fenwicke L. Holmes (1883–1973)

Christ Universal Temple (1956)
and Universal Foundation
for Better Living,
Chicago, IL (1974)
Johnnie Colemon (not available)

Hillside Chapel of Truth,
International and Barbara
King School of Ministry
Atlanta, GA (1971)
Barbara King (not available)

Seicho-No-Ie (1930)
Masaharu Taniguchi
(1893–1985)

The Evolution of the New Thought Movement

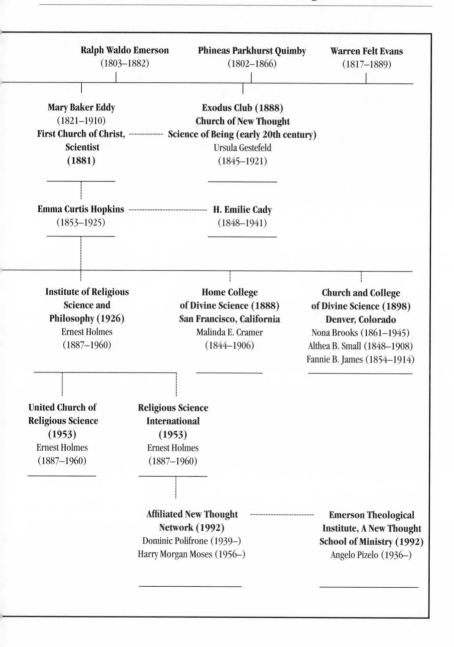

Ralph Waldo Emerson
(1803–1882)

Phineas Parkhurst Quimby
(1802–1866)

Warren Felt Evans
(1817–1889)

Mary Baker Eddy
(1821–1910)
First Church of Christ,
Scientist
(1881)

Exodus Club (1888)
Church of New Thought
Science of Being (early 20th century)
Ursula Gestefeld
(1845–1921)

Emma Curtis Hopkins
(1853–1925)

H. Emilie Cady
(1848–1941)

Institute of Religious
Science and
Philosophy (1926)
Ernest Holmes
(1887–1960)

Home College
of Divine Science (1888)
San Francisco, California
Malinda E. Cramer
(1844–1906)

Church and College
of Divine Science (1898)
Denver, Colorado
Nona Brooks (1861–1945)
Althea B. Small (1848–1908)
Fannie B. James (1854–1914)

United Church of
Religious Science
(1953)
Ernest Holmes
(1887–1960)

Religious Science
International
(1953)
Ernest Holmes
(1887–1960)

Affiliated New Thought
Network (1992)
Dominic Polifrone (1939–)
Harry Morgan Moses (1956–)

Emerson Theological
Institute, A New Thought
School of Ministry (1992)
Angelo Pizelo (1936–)

Notes

Introduction

1. Freeman, *The Household of Faith;* Bach, *The Unity Way of Life;* D'Andrade, *Charles Fillmore;* Vahle, *The Unity Movement;* Verderber, "The Rhetoric of Charles Fillmore."
2. Mead, *Handbook of Denominations in the United States;* Cerminara, *Insights for the Age of Aquarius;* Braden, *These Also Believe* and *Spirits in Rebellion;* Fischer, comp., *A Complete Concordance to the Published Writings of Charles Fillmore.*
3. Bormann, *Theory and Research in the Communicative Arts,* 175.
4. Fillmore, *Talks on Truth;* Fillmore and Schobert, *Metaphysical Bible Dictionary.*
5. Please note: throughout this volume, "Unity School of Christianity" and Unity are used interchangeably.
6. Holmes, *The Science of Mind,* 25.
7. Herrmann, *Sir John Templeton,* 152–53.

1. The Fillmores and the Origins of the Unity Movement

1. Except as otherwise cited, material for this section is taken from Charles Fillmore, "Confidentially," in Gatlin, *Unity's Fifty Golden Years,* x–xi.
2. Ibid., x.
3. D'Andrade, *Charles Fillmore,* 4.
4. Freeman, *Household of Faith,* 20–21.
5. D'Andrade, *Charles Fillmore,* 10.
6. Ibid., 9.
7. Freeman, *Household of Faith,* 28.
8. Except as otherwise cited, material for this section is taken from Gatlin, *Unity's Fifty Golden Years,* 3–4.
9. Freeman, *Household of Faith,* 42.
10. From *Guideposts,* reprinted in ibid.
11. Braden, *These Also Believe,* 131.
12. Freeman, *Household of Faith,* 42–43.
13. Braden, *These Also Believe,* 151.
14. Fillmore, *The Revealing Word,* s.v. "Metaphysics."
15. Hopkins, "Catalogue of Classes," 25.
16. Fillmore, "Emma Hopkins at Kansas City," 12.

17. Ibid.

18. Editorial in *Modern Thought,* November 1889; quoted in Freeman, *Household of Faith*, 43.

19. Hopkins, "Catalogue of Classes," 25.

20. Fillmore, "Our Mission," 10. All subsequent quotes are from this page as well.

21. Mead, *Handbook of Denominations*, 224.

22. Gatlin, *Unity's Fifty Golden Years*, 13.

23. Freeman, *Household of Faith*, 61–62.

24. Fillmore, "Society of Silent Help," 9 (emphasis added).

25. Ibid.

26. Jethro, "Healing Suggestions," 5.

27. "Extracts from Letters We Have Written," 3.

28. Dresser, "Dr. Quimby's Theory of Matter," 6.

29. Frances, "Pencil Jottings," 7.

30. "Each Member of Silent Unity," 9.

31. Gatlin, *Unity's Fifty Golden Years*, 45.

32. Cady, *Lessons in Truth, How I Used Truth,* and *God a Present Help.*

33. "Extract of a Letter to Myrtle Fillmore from Dr. H. Emilie Cady," 9.

34. Cady, *How I Used Truth*, 94–95.

35. For further explanation of the Word that was with God, and the way man uses his own *spoken word*, see appendix B, s.v. "Word."

36. "The Unity Viewpoint," 2–3.

37. Gatlin, *Unity's Fifty Golden Years*, 16–17.

38. "A Manual of Prayer," 8.

39. Gatlin, *Unity's Fifty Golden Years*, 28–29.

40. Ibid., 19; "Interesting Facts about Unity," 2.

41. Gatlin, *Unity's Fifty Golden Years*, 21.

42. "Unity Daily Word Heartily Received," 28.

43. Decker, ed., *Unity's Seventy Years of Faith and Works,* 83.

44. Rowland, "A Drill in the Silence" and "Come Ye Apart Awhile."

45. Myrtle Fillmore, "How I Found Health," in *Unity's Seventy Years of Faith and Works*, ed. Decker, 12.

46. Fillmore, "Heal the Sick," 10.

47. Rowland, *The Magic of the Word* (Unity Village, Mo.: Unity School of Christianity, 1968), 10.

48. Ibid., 12.

49. See, for example, "Prayers Are Answered," Unity School of Christianity booklet, Unity Village, Mo., 1972.

50. Vahle, *The Unity Movement*, 256.
51. Ibid., 259; Freeman, *Household of Faith*, 179–80.
52. Vahle, *The Unity Movement*, 315.
53. Lytton, *Understanding Unity for the Millions,* 140.
54. Bach, *The Unity Way of Life*, 52.
55. Bach, *Had You Been Born in Another Faith,* 171–72. Martin Luther's main objection to the Catholic Church was not based upon Scriptural difference, but upon liturgical differences and upon the sale of indulgences." See Mead, *Handbook of Denominations*, 133.
56. Bach, *Had You Been Born in Another Faith,* 36.
57. Mead, *Handbook of Denominations*, 209, 210.
58. Gatlin, *Unity's Fifty Golden Years*, 94; Fillmore and Schobert, *Metaphysical Bible Dictionary*, i. See appendix A for complete "Preface" and a description of Fillmore's criteria and methods of research.
59. Dessoir, *Aesthetics and Theory of Art,* 328; Meyer, "Unity and the Bible," 7.
60. Dr. Ernest C. Wilson, telephone interview with the author, Sept. 26, 1974.
61. Fillmore and Schobert, *Metaphysical Bible Dictionary*, ii.
62. Gatlin, *Unity's Fifty Golden Years*, 95.
63. Berry, "Unity School of Christianity in the Light of the Scriptures," 8.
64. *Encyclopedia of Religion and Ethics,* s.v. "Metaphysics." Emphasis added.
65. Dr. Ernest C. Wilson, minister of Kansas City Unity Society of Practical Christianity, personal letter to the author, Sept. 26, 1974.
66. Gatlin, *Unity's Fifty Golden Years*, 95.
67. See Corson, *The Voice and Spiritual Education* (New York: Macmillan, 1896).
68. Fillmore, *Mysteries of Genesis*, 56. Brackets appear in the text.
69. Fillmore, "The Adventure Called Unity," 6–7.
70. Gable, comp., "What It Means," ii–iii.
71. D'Andrade, *Charles Fillmore,* 142.
72. See, for example, Sloan, "Hermeneutics," 102; Marle, *Introduction to Hermeneutics;* and *The Interpreter's Bible* (New York: Abingdon Press, 1951).
73. Charles Fillmore, "Unity of Religion and Science," speech manuscript in *Unity's Seventy Years of Faith and Work,* ed. Decker, 110–11.
74. "A Thought Is Its Command."

2. The Unity Student and the Pursuit of Health

1. Reprinted from the *Handbook of Religion and Mental Health*, edited by Harold G. Koenig, "Religion and Mental Health from the Unity Perspective" by Glenn R. Mosley, copyright 1998, with permission from Elsevier.
2. Grof and Grof, eds., *Spiritual Emergency.*

3. Harvard Medical School, *Survey on Use of Alternative Medicine* (Cambridge: Harvard Medical School, 1993).

4. Association of Unity Churches, International, *Survey of 781 (of 960) Unity Ministers, Licensed Teachers, and Congregants* (Lee's Summit, Mo.: Association of Unity Churches, 1997). All further references to the Association of Unity Churches, International survey are to this source.

5. Dorsey, *Illness or Allness,* 445–46.

6. G. R. Mosley, *A Comparison of Secular and Religious Experiential Education Activities in the Adult Religious Education Classroom* (Ph.D. diss., Ohio State University, 1980).

7. Weil, "Can St. John's Wort Ease Depression?" 8.

8. Althoff, Williams, Molvig, and Schuster, *A Guide to Alternative Medicine.*

9. Murray, *Natural Alternatives to Prozac.*

10. D'Adamo, *Eat Right for Your Type.*

11. "Vital Signs," television transcript, Bonnie View Productions, New York, June 26, 1997.

12. Versau, "Religion Is Beneficial to Your Health," E1.

13. Reynolds, "Prayer the Medicine Patients Are Seeking," 10A.

14. Cohen, "The Greatest Story Never Told," 70.

15. Carey and Visgaitis, "Doctors Pray for Selves," 2A.

3. The Development of the New Thought Movement

1. Holmes, *The Science of Mind* (1997 ed.), 139.

2. Huxley, *The Perennial Philosophy,* vii.

3. Excerpted from Rev. Simeon Stefanidakis, "Forerunners to Modern Spiritualism: Emanuel Swedenborg (1688–1772)," www.fst.org/spirit2.htm, accessed Dec. 6, 2004.

4. *Melton Encyclopedia of American Religions,* 134.

5. Ibid.

6. "Ernest Holmes (1887–1960), Founder of the Religious Science Movement," abstracted from the booklet *Path of Discovery*, prepared by Scott Awbrey, Los Angeles United Church of Religious Science, 1987, http://ernestholmes.wwwhubs.com/.

7. Vahle, *Open at the Top,* 5.

8. Ibid., 1

9. James Reid, "Dr. Ernest Holmes: The First Religious Scientist," http://www.religiousscience.org/ucrs_site/our_founder/first_religious.html, accessed Dec. 12, 2004.

10. Ibid.

11. Holmes, *The Science of Mind* (1997 ed.), 458.

12. Vahle, *Open at the Top*, 7.

13. "Dr. Masaharu Taniguchi: The Miracle Man of Japan and the Origins of the Truth," www.snitruth.org/dr.htm.

14. From a report on the *Third Synthesis Dialogues, Rome, 2004,* submitted by Barbara Fields, Synthesis Dialogues Cofounder and Director.

15. Beckwith, *A Manifesto of Peace,* 42.

16. John Naisbitt and Patricia Aburdene, *Megatrends 2000: Ten New Directions for the 1990s* (New York: Morrow, 1990).

17. www.wisdomuniversity.org, accessed Feb. 15, 2005.

18. Vahle, *The Unity Movement,* 422.

19. Ibid., 423.

4. The Joint Search for Spiritual Truth by Modern Science and World Religion

1. Templeton and Hermann, *Is God the Only Reality?*, 9.

2. Barbour, *Religion and Science,* chap. 4.

3. Schilpp, ed., *Albert Einstein,* 659–60.

4. "The Spinoza Reference," Jan. 18, 1999, www.einsteinandreligion.com/Spinoza.html.

5. Lincoln, *The Universe and Dr. Einstein,* 118.

6. Loehr, *Science, Religion, and the Development of Religion as a Science.*

7. Grassie, letter to Dr. Vladislav Soskin.

8. Walter R. Hearn, "Evidence of Purpose in the Universe," in *Evidence of Purpose,* ed. Templeton, 58.

9. Pierre Teilhard de Chardin, *The Phenomenon of Man* (New York: Harper Perennial, 1976).

10. NASA, ESA, Y. Izotov, and T. Thuan, "Hubble Uncovers a Baby Galaxy in a Grown-up Universe," Hubblesite, Dec. 1, 2004, http://hubblesite.org/newscenter/newsdesk/archive/releases/2004/35/, accessed Oct. 31, 2005.

11. Burhoe, "The Human Prospect and the Lord of History," 299.

12. Henderson, "Can Scientists and Theologians Be Friends?"

13. Mosley and Hill, *The Power of Prayer around the World,* 77–82.

5. Helping the World's Great Religions Grow

1. Varadaraja Raman, *Meta* 103 (May 1998), www.metanexus.net.

2. Henry Simon, "Visitors Can Feel Like VIPs When You Use the Phone,"

Action Information, May/June 1992, published by the Alban Institute, Herndon, Va.

3. Roy Oswald, "How Do You Make Your Church More Inviting?" *Action Information*, Jan./Feb. 1992, published by the Alban Institute, Herndon, Va.

4. Glenn Mosley, "Can I . . . Will I . . . Can I?" *Contact Magazine* (Aug./Sept. 1993), published by the Association of Unity Churches.

Appendix A. *Preface of the* Metaphysical Bible Dictionary

1. From the *Metaphysical Bible Dictionary* by Charles Fillmore, originally published in 1931, reprinted with permission from the Unity School of Christianity, Unity Village, Mo.

Appendix B. *Selections from the* Metaphysical Bible Dictionary

1. From the *Metaphysical Bible Dictionary* by Charles Fillmore, originally published in 1931, reprinted with permission from the Unity School of Christianity, Unity Village, Mo.

Appendix C. *Charles Fillmore in His Own Words*

1. Radio transcript and radio talk, used by permission, were first published in *A Modern Way-Shower*, booklet comp. by editorial staff, Unity Books, Unity Village, Mo., 1974, 21–25, 55–64, respectively.

Selected Bibliography

Books

Althoff, S., P. Williams, D. Molvig, and L. Schuster. *A Guide to Alternative Medicine*. Lincolnwood, Ill.: Publications International, 1997.

Anderson, C. Alan, and Deborah G. Whitehouse. *New Thought: A Practical American Spirituality*. New York: Crossroad, 1995.

Bach, Marcus. *Had You Been Born in Another Faith*. Englewood Cliffs, N.J.: Prentice-Hall, 1961.

——. *The Unity Way of Life*. Englewood Cliffs, N.J.: Prentice-Hall, 1962.

Bahn, Eugene, and Margaret L. Bahn. *A History of Oral Interpretation*. Minneapolis: Burgess, 1971.

Barbour, Ian. *Religion and Science: Historical and Contemporary Issues*. San Francisco: HarperCollins, 1997.

Beckwith, Michael. *A Manifesto of Peace*. Culver City, Calif.: Agape Publishing, 2002.

Beebe, Tom. *Who's Who in New Thought*. Lakewood, Ga.: CSA Press, 1977.

Bormann, Ernest G. *Theory and Research in the Communicative Arts*. New York: Holt, Rinehart, & Winston, 1965.

Braden, Charles S. *Spirits in Rebellion: The Rise and Development of New Thought*. Dallas: Southern Methodist University Press, 1963.

——. *These Also Believe*. New York: Macmillan, 1950.

Cady, H. Emilie. *God a Present Help*. Kansas City, Mo.: Unity School of Christianity, 1940.

——. *How I Used Truth*. Kansas City, Mo.: Unity School of Christianity, 1916.

——. *Lessons in Truth*. Kansas City, Mo.: Unity Book Co., 1894.

Cerminara, Gina. *Insights for the Age of Aquarius*. Englewood Cliffs, N.J.: Prentice-Hall, 1973.

Clayton, Philip, and Arthur Peacocke, eds. *In Whom We Live and Move and Have Our Being: Panentheistic Reflections on God's Presence in a Scientific World*. Grand Rapids, Mich.: Eerdmans, 2004.

Colemon, Johnnie. *Open Your Mind and Be Healed*. Camarillo, Calif.: DeVorss & Co., 2000.

Connors, Sharon. *Adventures in Prayer: Praying Your Way to a God You Can Trust*. New York: Bantam Books, 2004.

Corson, Hiram. *The Voice and Spiritual Education*. New York: Macmillan, 1896.

D'Adamo, P. J. *Eat Right for Your Type*. New York: Putnam, 1996.

D'Andrade, Hugh. *Charles Fillmore: Herald of the New Age*. New York: Harper & Row, 1974.

Decker, James A., ed. *Unity's Seventy Years of Faith and Works*. Lee's Summit, Mo.: Unity School of Christianity, 1959.

Dessoir, Max. *Aesthetics and Theory of Art*. Translated by Stephen A. Emery. Detroit: Wayne State University Press, 1970.

Dorsey, J. M. *Illness or Allness: Conversations of a Psychiatrist*. Detroit: Wayne State University Press, 1965.

Dresser, Horatio W. *A History of the New Thought Movement*. New York: Thomas Y. Crowell Co., 1919.

Encyclopedia of Religion and Ethics. New York: Scribner & Sons, n.d., s.v. "Metaphysics," vol. XVIII.

Fillmore, Charles. *Dynamics for Living*. Edited by Warren Meyer. Lee's Summit, Mo.: Unity Books, 1967.

———. *Jesus Christ Heals*. Kansas City, Mo.: Unity School of Christianity, 1939.

———. *Mysteries of Genesis*. Rev. ed. Kansas City, Mo.: Unity School of Christianity, 1944.

———. *Mysteries of John*. Kansas City, Mo.: Unity School of Christianity, 1946.

———. *Prosperity*. Kansas City, Mo.: Unity School of Christianity, 1936.

———. *The Revealing Word*. Edited by staff. Lee's Summit, Mo.: Unity Books, 1961.

———. *Talks on Truth*. Kansas City, Mo.: Unity School of Christianity, 1926.

Fillmore, Charles, and Theodosia Schobert. *Metaphysical Bible Dictionary*. Kansas City, Mo.: Unity School of Christianity, 1931.

Fillmore, Myrtle. *Letters of Myrtle Fillmore*. Edited by Frances W. Foulks. Kansas City, Mo.: Unity School of Christianity, 1936.

Fischer, Jeffrey, comp. *A Complete Concordance to the Published Writings of Charles Fillmore*. Unity Village, Mo.: Unity Books, 1975.

Fox, Emmet. *Sermon on the Mount*. Rev. ed. San Francisco: HarperCollins, 1989.

Fox, Matthew. *Original Blessing*. Santa Fe, N.M.: Bear & Company, 1983.

Freeman, James Dillet. *The Household of Faith*. Lee's Summit, Mo.: Unity School of Christianity, 1951.

Gaither, James. *The Essential Charles Fillmore*. Unity Village, Mo.: Unity Books, 1999.

Gatlin, Dana. *The Story of Unity's Fifty Golden Years*. Kansas City, Mo.: Unity School of Christianity, 1939.

Grof, S., and C. Grof, eds. *Spiritual Emergency: When Personal Transformation Becomes a Crisis*. Los Angeles: Tarcher, 1989.

Herrmann, Robert L. *Sir John Templeton*. Philadelphia, Pa.: Templeton Foundation Press, 1998.

Holmes, Ernest. *The Science of Mind: A Philosophy, a Faith, a Way of Life*. New York: Penguin Putnam, 1997.

Hopkins, Emma Curtis. *High Mysticism*. Cornwall Bridge, Conn.: High Watch Fellowship, 1892.

Huxley, Aldous. *The Perennial Philosophy*. New York: Harper Colophon Books, 1944.

The Interpreter's Bible. New York: Abingdon Press, 1951.

Judah, J. Stillson. *The History and Philosophy of the Metaphysical Movements in America*. Philadelphia: Westminster Press, 1957.

King, Barbara L. *The Church: A Matter of Consciousness*. Atlanta: Barbara King Ministries, 1980.

——. *What Is a Miracle?* Atlanta: Barbara King Ministries, 1981.

Koenig, Harold G., ed. *Handbook of Religion and Mental Health*. New York: Academic Press, 1998.

Larson, Martin A. *New Thought Religion*. New York: Philosophical Library, 1987.

Lincoln, Barnett. *The Universe and Dr. Einstein*. New York: Signet, 1948.

Loehr, Franklin. *Science, Religion, and the Development of Religion as a Science*. Grand Island, Fla: Gnosticours, Ltd., 1983.

Lytton, Kam. *Understanding Unity for the Millions*. Los Angeles: Sherbourne Press, 1969.

Marle, Rene. *Introduction to Hermeneutics*. New York: Herder and Herder, 1967.

Mead, Frank S. *Handbook of Denominations in the United States*. 2nd rev. ed. New York: Abingdon Press, 1961.

Mosley, Glenn R. *Unity Methods of Self-Exploration*. Detroit: Ducat Publishing, 1975.

Mosley, Glenn R., and Joanna Hill. *The Power of Prayer Around the World*. Philadelphia: Templeton Foundation Press, 2000.

Murray, M. T. *Natural Alternatives to Prozac*. New York: Morrow, 1996.

Naisbitt, John, and Patricia Aburdene. *Megatrends 2000: Ten New Directions for the 1990s*. New York: Morrow, 1990.

Naisbitt, John, and Patricia Aburdene. *Megatrends 2000*. New York: Morrow, 1983.

Peale, Norman Vincent. *Power of Positive Thinking*. New York: Prentice-Hall, 1952.

Quimby, Phineas Parkhurst. *The Healing Wisdom of Dr. P. P. Quimby*. Edited by Mason Alonzo Clark. Los Altos, Calif.: Frontal Lobe Publishers, 1982.

Rowland, May. *Dare to Believe*. Lee's Summit, Mo.: Unity School of Christianity, 1961.

————. *The Magic of the Word*. Unity Village, Mo.: Unity Books, 1972.

Schilpp, Paul Arthur, ed. *Albert Einstein: Philosopher-Scientist*. 3rd ed. LaSalle, Ill.: Open Court Publishing, 1970.

Stuber, Stanley I. *How We Got Our Denominations*. New York: Association Press, 1927.

Templeton, John Marks. *Agape Love: A Tradition Found in Eight World Religions*. Philadelphia, Pa.: Templeton Foundation Press, 1999.

Templeton, John Marks, ed. *Evidence of Purpose*. New York: Continuum, 1994.

Templeton, John Marks, and Robert L. Herrmann. *Is God the Only Reality?* New York: Continuum, 1994.

Templeton, Sir John, and Rebekah Alezander Dunlap. *Why Are We Created: Increasing Our Understanding of Humanity's Purpose on Earth*. Philadelphia, Pa.: Templeton Foundation Press, 2003.

Vahle, Neal. *Open at the Top: The Life of Ernest Holmes*. Mill Valley, Calif.: Open View Press, 1993.

————. *Torch-Bearer to Light the Way: The Life of Myrtle Fillmore*. Mill Valley, Calif.: Open View Press, 1996.

————. *The Unity Movement: Its Evolution and Spiritual Teachings*. Philadelphia: Templeton Foundation Press, 2002.

Wilber, Ken. *The Simple Feeling of Being: Embracing Your True Nature*. Boston: Shamballa Publications, 2004.

Periodicals and Pamphlets

Berry, Harold J. "Unity School of Christianity in the Light of the Scriptures" (pamphlet). Back to the Bible, Lincoln, Neb., 1964.

Burhoe, R. "The Human Prospect and the Lord of History." *Zygon: Journal of Religion and Science* 10 (1975): 299.

Carey, A., and G. Visgaitis. "Doctors Pray for Selves." *USA Today*, March 27, 1997, 2A.

Cohen, J. "The Greatest Story Never Told." *Utne Reader* (March/April 1997): 70.

Dresser, Horatio W. "Dr. Quimby's Theory of Matter." *Unity*, Oct. 15, 1895, 6-7.

"Each Member of Silent Unity." *Unity*, May 1892, 9.

"Extract of a Letter to Myrtle Fillmore from Dr. H. Emilie Cady." *Unity*, March 1892, 9.

"Extracts from Letters We Have Written." *Unity*, September 1891, 3.

Fillmore, Charles R. "The Adventure Called Unity" (pamphlet). Unity School of Christianity, Lee's Summit, Mo., 1967.

Fillmore, Charles. "Heal the Sick" (pamphlet). Unity School of Christianity, Lee's Summit, Mo., 1968.

Fillmore, Charles. "Emma Hopkins at Kansas City." *Modern Thought*, Nov. 1889, 12.

Fillmore, Charles. "Our Mission." *Modern Thought,* April 1889, 10.

Fillmore, Lowell. "They Made a Contract with God." *Guideposts,* Sept. 1948, 23–25.

Fillmore, Myrtle. "Society of Silent Help." *Modern Thought*, May 1890, 9.

Frances, "Pencil Jottings," *Unity*, Oct. 15, 1895, 7.

Henderson, Stephen. "Can Scientists and Theologians Be Friends?" *Milestones*, (November 2004).

"Interesting Facts about Unity." *Unity Service Bulletin,* January 1923, 2.

Jethro. "Healing Suggestions." *Modern Thought*, April 1889, 5.

"A Manual of Prayer" (pamphlet). Unity School of Christianity, Unity Village, Mo., 1970.

Meyer, Louis E. "Unity and the Bible" (pamphlet). Unity School of Christianity, Lee's Summit, Mo., 1967.

Reynolds, B. "Prayer the Medicine Patients Are Seeking." *USA Today,* May 3, 1996, 10A.

Rowland, May. "Come Ye Apart Awhile" (pamphlet). Unity School of Christianity, Lee's Summit, Mo., 1957.

————. "A Drill in the Silence" (pamphlet). Unity School of Christianity, Lee's Summit, Mo., 1968.

Sloan, Thomas O. "Hermeneutics: The Interpreter's House Revisited." Reviews of Richard E. Palmer, *Hermeneutics: Interpretation Theory in Schleiermacher, Dilthey, Heidegger, and Gadamer,* and E. D. Hirsch Jr., *Validity in Interpretation*, in *Quarterly Journal of Speech* 58 (Feb. 1971): 102–18.

"A Thought Is Its Command." *Detroit Free Press,* June 29, 1974.

"Truth Bows at No Human Shrine." *Modern Thought*, June 1889, 9.

"Unity Daily Word Heartily Received." *Unity*, Sept. 1924, 28.

Versau, J. "Religion Is Beneficial to Your Health." *Chicago Sun Times,* March 29, 1997, E1.

Weil, A. "Can St. John's Wort Ease Depression?" *Self-Healing* (July 1997): 3–4.

Whitehouse, Deb. "God: Personal, Eternal, and New." *Unity Magazine,* April 1996.

Unpublished Materials

Gable, Francis J., comp. "What It Means" (typewritten). Unity School of Christianity, Kansas City, Mo., 1942.

Hartung, Nancy. "The Contributions of Hiram Corson to the Field of Oral Interpretation." M.A. thesis, Wayne State University, Detroit, 1963.

Hopkins, Emma Curtis. "Catalogue of Classes" (typewritten). Christian Science Theological Seminary, Chicago, 1887.

Teener, James W. "Thesis on Unity School of Christianity." Ph.D. diss., University of Chicago, 1939.

"The Unity Viewpoint" (radio transcript). Unity School of Christianity, Lee's Summit, Mo., June 20, 1959.

Verderber, Rudolph F. "The Rhetoric of Charles Fillmore." Ph.D. diss., University of Missouri, Columbia, Mo., 1962.

Whaley, Harold Barton. "Collection and Preservation of the Materials of the New Thought Movement." Master's thesis, University of Missouri-Kansas City, Kansas City, Mo., 1973.

White, Phillip. "A Study of New Thought as a Lay Movement: Some Implications." M.Div. essay, St. Paul School of Theology (Methodist), Kansas City, Mo., 1972.

Index